KUMBAYA

Griffin Lotson

Sierra Leonean Writers Series

"Kumbaya"

First Published 2019
Revised edition 2022

Printed in Sierra Leone, West Africa
and Darien, Georgia. USA

ISBN: 978-16595-02-54-1

Sierra Leonean Writers Series (SLWS)
Warima, Freetown, Accra
Publisher: Prof. Osman Sankoh (Mallam O.)
Publisher@sl-writers-series.org
www.sl-writers-series.org

Content

Acknowledgments

I want to give a very special thanks to Editor Jim Morrison. Without his assistance and help this book, "Kumbaya", would not be possible. As the author of this book, I have several special sets of skills. Unfortunately, writing is not one of those special skills, so I approached my friend Jim to help me with this book. I had read many of Jim's articles that he had written in the past; therefore I approached him about assisting with this book. He agreed, and as they say, the rest is history.

Jim Morrison has a lifetime of writing and editing experience. Jim majored in journalism at the University of Georgia, graduating with an arts bachelor in journalism. Jim edited and wrote for the former Georgia State Game and Fish Commission's award winning monthly magazine, ghost writing statements for the Commission's director, Georgia Governor Carl Sanders, and Jimmy Carter on conservation subjects. Now retired, Jim still leads by assisting me with this book, including another book, "Gullah Geechee 101".

Very special thanks to" Nettie Evans" for her time and experience as an educator in editing a great portion of this book.

There are many others that have contributed to this very special one of a kind book ,each of you know who you are, and I thank you for your part in this book, that is the only book every printed in history called "Kumbaya." I am certain I cannot name everyone who helped with this very special project and book, so thanks to each of you who are part of my family and friends that helped makes this book possible. Many of you will be named in the contents of this book, and as the author Griffin Lotson travel and lecture. Wife Carolyn, my three children: Griffin Lamar, Montrell and Carlinda. I thank everyone for making this book "Kumbaya" possible.**(I can't wait to see the first Movie or Play of "Kumbaya")**

Congratulations
Sierra Leone, West Africa

Congratulations to the first company and publisher to publish the first Book on "Kumbaya". A West Africa Sierra Leone, Publisher, Professor Osman Sankoh (Mallam O.) with their Publishing Company: Sierra Leonean Writers Series (SLWS). The author of the first book in the world with a subject title "Kumbaya". The author has hand-picked the publisher and the publishing company because of its great philanthropic work to promote the West African country of Sierra Leone, The author Griffin Lotson is a direct descendent of Sierra Leone, and Lotson was birth into the Gullah Geechee culture.

 Griffin Lotson the author has traced his ancestral roots DNA to Sierra Leone and the region. This is his way of giving back to the motherland West Africa in particular Sierra Leone where he Lotson knows a portion of the contributions from the sales of the "Kumbaya" book will be donated back to help other inspiring historians, writers and Sierra Leone to publish their own book and learning materials.

 A short list to show some of the citizens and Government officials in Sierra Leone that has supported the author Griffin Lotson work.

First Lady of Sierra Leone: Fatima Maada Bio, William Ikrobinson, Ministry of Culture and Tourism, Chairman of Monuments and Relics, Charlie Hefner, Amadu Massally, Augustine Bockarie, Isatu Smith, Isatu Isha Sillah, Ibrahim V. Kondoh, John K. Ansumana, Osman B. Sessay, and others from Serra Leone, West Africa

Kumbaya: History of an Old Song

Ninety three years of work (1926-2019) finally gave birth to this book about a song that literally had its birth in a little place on the planet earth called Darien, Georgia, and now has made its way into the world's lexicon.

This book with this subject, is the first of its kind written anywhere in the world and is simply titled "Kumbaya." In this book we have built a strong partnership and collaboration with the United States of America Library of Congress and some of its officials. We have combined our efforts to; hopefully, give you a more accurate picture of the history of this internationally known song that has become a very popular and famous phrase. Most of us if not all of us have said the word "Kumbaya." Just think about it, how many people do you know that have not heard the word "Kumbaya" or sung "Kumbaya"? If you're over the age of 30, the chances are you know or have sung some part of "Kumbaya." About 50 to 80 per cent of the people you know have used or said the word "Kumbaya" for good reasons and sometimes for bad reasons. That in itself makes it the world's most talked about song or phrase. "Kumbaya" is known internationally by over one billion individuals as the song has crossed all cultural, racial, and ethnic groups of people anywhere on the planet earth. The word is now in our lexicon, at first in a very good way as a call for divine help, let us all come together for unity, holding hands to show that we all need each other if we want to succeed. Then it took a sharp turn in a negative direction. Some of us, but not all, started using the same words in a negative way, as a sign of weakness, making fun of others or gatherings.

It is an African American spiritual, "Kumbaya", also known by other titles such as "Kumbayah," "Come By Ya," and "Come By Here." In the years since this article was first published, we've learned some more about the origin of the song and some other new developments have occurred. In particular as a Federal Commissioner on the Gullah Geechee Cultural Heritage Commission and as the Mayor Pro Tem of the City of Darien, Georgia, I have had the honor of spearheading a successful effort to get the song recognized as the official State Historical Song of Georgia. The Georgia Senate passed the resolution. In February 2017, and in addition to that, the United States of America's Congress, with the combined efforts of myself and many friends, with my initiation, pushed and drove to bring the song Kumbaya to a greater worldwide official recognition, and it now added to American history and to world history recognition as the first known recording in the world, from a place called Darien, Georgia.

Kumbaya

According to the editor and owner of the Darien News, Kathleen Russell: "Two Darien Men bring "Kumbaya" to be world's song asking for divine intervention."

Robert Winslow Gordon

Griffin Lotson

Robert Winslow Gordon and Griffin Lotson have forever changed the history of the world's most popular song. The information on the song's history in the resolution was provided to the State legislature by Lotson with Senator William Ligon taking the lead with the information and the idea of how maybe we can make Georgia history, "The State of Georgia's first Historical Song". Using the accomplishment of achieving new Georgia history, we took those findings to Washington, DC to our elected legislator, U.S. Congressman Buddy Carter of Georgia's 1st District, hoping he could help us push to get congressional recognition, and from that we achieved what some would say was impossible, to get national recognition from Congress. We did, and we leveraged that experience to get international recognition on a worldwide level. In more detail in this book, we will show more information on how we made all this happen.

Stephen Winick, an independent researcher, is a great historian and contributor to the Library of Congress. In the early part of 2018, Stephen and I combined our efforts and communicated with the New York Times for a very special news article concerning Kumbaya. From that conversation, I feel privileged that Stephen included some of the recent new history in one of his Library of Congress articles. We will share some of it with you in this book from the earlier version of this article.

"Kumbaya," once one of the most popular songs in the folk revival, has more recently fallen on hard times. In the early 1980s, something happened. "Kumbaya" became the English-speaking world's favorite folk song to ridicule, the musical metaphor for corny camaraderie. An extensive (and we do mean extensive) search of databases of newspapers, magazines, and other sources turned up what may be the first ironic reference to "Kumbaya" in print, from August 16, 1985.

The line is from a Washington Post review by Rita Kempley of the comedy movie "Volunteers:" "Tom Hanks and John Candy make war on the Peace Corps in `Volunteers,' a belated lampoon of `60s altruism and the idealistic young Kumbayahoos who went off to save the Third World." How did she settle on "Kumbaya"? Had she heard others mocking it? Was it something about the cynicism felt by liberals under Reagan? A commentary about the religious theme of the song, at a time when the Moral Majority was making its name? Kempley can't remember. "I guess that song was the ultimate expression of people in the 60s who really cared," said Kemply.

And then everyone decided, "let's just make fun of that." Dissing, disrespecting "Kumbaya" caught on. In 1988, a column in The Christian Science Monitor knocked a New Age performance: "Next he'll want you to sing `Kumbaya.'... Time to leave." In 1994, then senatorial candidate Rick Santorum dismissed the federal AmeriCorps program as "somebody ... going to do one year of community service picking up trash in a park and singing `Kumbaya' around the campfire." These days, a search for "Kumbaya" on the internet is almost as likely to turn up as a joke, rather than the song in a positive light.

In its heyday, "Kumbaya" from the 1950s through the 1990s was recorded by dozens of artists, including Joan Baez, the Weavers, Odetta, Pete Seeger, Sweet Honey in the Rock, Nanci Griffith, and Raffi in the United States; Joan Orleans in Germany; MandaDjinn in France; the Seekers in Australia; and many others around the world. However, overlapping with that heyday, from the 1980s through the 2000s, the song experienced a backlash. Musically, it came to be thought of as a children's campfire song, too simple or too silly for adults to bother with. Politically, it became shorthand for weak consensus seeking that fails to accomplish crucial goals. Socially, it came to stand for the touchy-feely, the wishy-washy, and the nerdy,

These recent attitudes toward the song are unfortunate, since the original is a beautiful example of traditional music, dialect, and creativity. However, the song's recent fall from grace has at least added some colorful metaphors to American political discourse, such phrases as "to join hands and sing 'Kumbaya,'" which means to ignore our differences and get along, and "Kumbaya moment," an event at which such naïve bonding occurs.

The First "Kumbay Moment"

Regardless of the song's fluctuating connotations, one question has long fascinated scholars: what was the first "Kumbaya moment?" In other words, where and when does the song come from? To answer this question, there's no better resource than the American Folklife Center Archive at the Library of Congress (AFC).

The song's early history is very well documented in the Archive, which includes the first known sound recordings of the song and probably the earliest manuscript copy as well. In addition, the Archive's subject file on the song (which gives it the title "Kum Ba Yah") contains rare documents pertaining to the song's history. Several researchers, most notably and recently Chee Hoo Lum, at the time a doctoral student in music education at the University of Washington, have used the Archive's resources to tell the story of the song. (Lum's article appeared in KodalyEnvoy, 33(3): pp5-11.).

However, the recent rediscovery of two versions at AFC—a manuscript taken down in 1926 and a cylinder recording made in the same year—makes a more complete account possible and helps dispel some common fallacies about the song.

One of these common misconceptions was espoused and spread by the song's first appearances in the folk revival. The first revival recording of the song, which called it "Kum Ba Yah," was released in 1958 by an Ohio-based group, the Folksmiths. In the liner notes, they claimed that the song came from Africa, and presented as evidence a previous claim that the song had been collected from missionaries in Angola. On the other hand, some scholars have located the origin of "Kumbaya" in the work of an Anglo-American composer and evangelist named Marvin Frey. In 1939, Frey published and copyrighted sheet music for one version of the song, which he called "Come by Here." Once "Kumbaya" was established as a standard of the folk revival, he pointed to his 1939 publication and claimed to have written the song; many commentators, including such publications as the New York Times, have chosen to believe his claim.

This means that during the early years of the folk revival, there were two widely believed theories of the song's origin (one ascribing it to black Africans and the other to a white American), and that both of these theories have persisted among some commentators to this day. As we shall see, in light of AFC's two early documents, neither of these theories is likely.

The most common claim made today about the origins of "Kumbaya" is that it is from the Gullah Geechee people of coastal Georgia and South Carolina. The fact that "ya" means "here" in Gullah, a Gullah origin is certainly possible, and is closer to the truth than either of the previous theories, but AFC's archival versions also make the Gullah claim more than certain. As the international Gullah Geechee lead consultant and historian of the song "Kumbaya", I have been able to verify and authenticate that the American Folklife Life Center of The Library of Congress's assumptions are accurate. In fact the term "come by ya" is a Gullah Geechee term that has evolved and made its way into the America Lexicon and now in the world's lexicon as "Kumbaya".

The Boyd Manuscript

One of the earliest records of "Kumbaya" in the AFC archive is in a manuscript sent to Robert Winslow Gordon, the Archive's founder, in 1927. The collector was Julian Parks Boyd, at that time a high school principal in Alliance, North Carolina. This version, which Boyd collected from his student Minnie Lee in 1926, was given the title "Oh, Lord, Won't You Come By Here," which is also the song's refrain.

Each verse is one line repeated three times, followed by this refrain: "Somebody's sick, Lord, come by here," "Somebody's dying, Lord, come by here," and "Somebody's in trouble, Lord, come by here." Although Boyd collected only the words, this structure is enough to mark Lee's performance as an early version of the well-known "Kumbaya."

I have copies of the student Minnie Lee's and Boyd's letters to Robert W. Gordon, given to me from the Library of Congress, to assist me in uncovering some of the hidden mysteries of "Kumbaya".

Student Minnie Lee's version of "Kumbaya" leads us to one of the many interesting stories hidden in the AFC archive: that of folklore collector Julian Parks Boyd. Boyd, who earned a master's degree from Duke University in 1926, spent only one school year, 1926-1927, at his job as a school teacher in Alliance. During that time, he showed a remarkable interest in folk song. From letters he sent to Gordon (now also in the AFC archive), we know that Boyd used a time-honored method among academic folklorists: he had his students collect traditional songs from their friends and families in the rural community around the school.

Although he was apparently quite selective, keeping only those songs he deemed true folk songs and discarding the rest, he amassed a collection of over a hundred songs, from which he created a typed manuscript. Boyd knew of Gordon through his columns in Adventure magazine, and sent the manuscript to him for his advice and comments in February, 1927. By March, Boyd's program of collecting folk songs had encountered a serious obstacle, and that, among other things, convinced him to leave Alliance for graduate school. "The school board and the community in general seem to think that collecting folk songs is an obnoxious practice, for some uncertain reason. The seniors were righteously indignant—it was the one thing that had thoroughly aroused their interest," he wrote to Gordon on March 30. "This particular school board fits Woodrow Wilson's definition of a board: 'long, wooden, and narrow,'" he continued. "And that explains why I am going to pursue my doctorate at Pennsylvania next year."

Boyd's departure for the University of Pennsylvania probably marked the end of his work as a folk song collector, but it was the beginning of a distinguished career as a historian and librarian. He eventually served as head librarian and professor of history at Princeton University, as the founding treasurer of the Society of American Archivists, and as president of the American Historical Association (1964). As an historian, he is best known as the editor of a definitive edition of the papers of Thomas Jefferson.

Before he left to take up the mantle of history, however, Boyd spent one more brief period as a folklorist. In his March 30 letter to Gordon, Boyd alludes to plans for a summer field trip to collect folk songs in the Outer Banks. The trip was sponsored by Professor Frank C. Brown of Duke University, then president of the North Carolina Folklore Society.

Although the correspondence from Boyd to Gordon terminates before the trip was to have started, we have no reason to think the trip was canceled. Furthermore, the Society's collection, later published as the seven-volume Frank C. Brown Collection of North Carolina Folklore, contains many items collected by Boyd, including the same version of "Kumbaya" that Boyd sent to Gordon. It has been overlooked by previous scholars of the history of the song, undoubtedly because its title, "Oh, Lord, Won't You Come By Here," bears little resemblance to the more familiar title, "Kumbaya."

Boyd sent his manuscript collection to Gordon in Georgia, before Gordon moved to Washington, D.C. and founded the Archive of American Folksong—which is now the American Folklife Center Archive. Gordon brought the manuscript with him to Washington, where it was among the original materials deposited in the Archive in 1928. Thus, from the very inception of the Archive, it contained at least one version of this classic song.

Robert Winslow Gordon and Henry Wylie

The two principle individuals who made the song Kumbaya historically famous are Robert Winslow Gordon and Henry Wylie. Robert Winslow Gordon was the first head of the Archive of American Folksong, which is now the American Folklife Center Archive. Henry Wiley has been given credit for being the singer of the world's oldest known recording of Kumbaya. Put these two individuals together, and they actually are the history makers of this song worldwide. For the sake of this book and history, in 1926 the name of the singer was given as H. Wylie. Now after much research, we have determined that his actual first name is Henry, and the actual spelling of his last name may have been Wylly. This was discovered after researching family records, cemetery records, and oral interviews from his cousins. My research in these matters was verified by finding out the Library of Congress expert Chris Smith with his research discovered some of the same information I had discovered using some of the same methods for researching but not all,. Not to brag, but I do have one more insight, and that is, I live in the area where the local descendants still live, so in the 90s I had one-on-one, face-to-face experiences and was able to collect some great oral history that I could use and match with written history to match the two pieces together and show proof of the facts to be placed in history. The Boyd papers make it clear that "Kumbaya" was represented in the Archive's very first collections. More surprisingly, a sound recording of the song was also among the archive's initial holdings, a fact that until now has been difficult to establish with certainty. Among the original materials in the AFC Archive were four cylinder recordings of spirituals with the refrain "come by here" or "come by yuh," collected by Gordon himself during his trips to Georgia from 1926 to 1928.

Gordon was convinced all four songs were related, and cross-referenced them when he made a card catalog for his manuscripts and cylinders. Subsequently, one of the four cylinders was broken, and one was lost, so two remain in the Archive. However, without hearing the cylinders, it would be impossible to state with certainty whether either was a version of "Kumbaya". As far as we know, this cylinder is the earliest sound recording of the song, and it is therefore among the most significant evidence on the song's early history. You can download it over the internet online, from the Library of Congress.

Robert Winslow Gordon's Catalog Card Index

On the original index card at the Library of Congress the song is identified as "Come By Here." The singer is identified only as H. Wylie. With now new research and new findings, H. Wylie is now known as Henry Wiley. (The spelling of the last name Wylie is spelled also as Wiley and or Wylly. The place where it was recorded was unknown from 1926 up until the year 2011 when I conducted my own research of the song and listened to the song, which I discovered was recorded in the original Gullah Geechee dialect. But most of the words on the scratchy recording are in understandable Gullah Geechee English, sung in a much higher pitch and must faster pace than the song is usually sung today.

I'm a seventh generation Gullah Geechee, so it was second nature when I heard the words. I knew right then it was recorded in Darien, Georgia, but up until that moment, even at the Library of Congress in Washington, DC, the place was not identified at all, but during this period, Gordon was living in Darien in 1926. Gordon rarely collected more than a few hours from there. Ironically, my grandfather, Robert Lotson, was recorded in 1926 by Gordon not too far from Darien. I discovered this knowledge of my grandfather's recording from the Library of Congress in Washington that I ordered and was shipped to me through Federal Express in August of 2012.

No one in my family for nearly a century (88 years) had ever talked about the recording, and I would venture to say my grandfather, Robert Lotson, did not know the song would be of any significance in the 21st-century.

My grandfather died in the 1970's. I knew him well. He lived to be a ripe old age, in his 90s. I had no knowledge at all of my grandfather singing for Mr. Gordon in 1926. Just think, the world's most popular song that's known by over one billion individuals all over the planet and my grandfather were recorded by Mr. Gordon at the same time as the famous "Kumbaya" song which was sung by another Gullah Geechee by the name of Henry Wylie, who lived in the same place as my grandfather, Robert Lotson, in a small community called Carneghan just north of Darien. My grandfather was born in 1882 in the same county in Georgia (McIntosh County). I'll talk more about this later in this book.

Robert Lotson Sr. 1882 – 1979. Recorded by Robert Winslow Gordon April 18, 1926, one day after the now famous "Kumbaya song.

For all of the history buffs who love doing research such as I do, you would find it interesting that my grandfather Robert Lotson was recorded one day after the very famous "Kumbaya" at the Library of Congress where he can be found on Robert Winslow Gordon cylinder A393 item number: GA161. The name of the song is "Sweet Water Rolling" recorded April 18, 1926 in Carneghan, Georgia. He was 44 years of age at the time of the recording on April 18, 1926.

The famous "Kumbaya" (Come By Here) song cylinder is numbered A389 and "Georgia 156." The cylinder is undated, but all the dated items in Gordon's numbering system from A290 to A434 are from April, 1926; the last precisely dated cylinder before "Come By Here" is dated April 15th, and the first after it is dated May 3rd, so from the written evidence, it appears the song was recorded within that two-week period.

This suspicion became clear to me and is confirmed by the cylinder itself. At the end of the cylinder, Wylie's voice faintly says something in Gullah Geechee words, which appears to be his name and date of the recording: "Sung by Henry Wylie, Darien, Georgia, April the seventeenth...."

Word for word match in Henry Wylie's Gullah Geechee Dialect

In this book I particularly want to follow an example of the song that was clearly distributed from the Library of Congress by Stephen Winick. My reasoning for that is Stephen had translated the original words into plain English. I thought it would be fitting with the new knowledge that it was in actuality Gullah Geechee words mixed with English words, that we would give the true essence and true history of the words as they were sung in the original dialect of Gullah Geechee. I wanted the words to be historically correct as Henry Wylie was singing the song word for word in his own language/dialect.

Now for the first time anywhere it would be printed word for word as close as we could possibly match in Henry Wylie's Gullah Geechee dialect (to him, his language). Now we have done so for the first time back in 2012, so I'm placing the words below.

The first draft musical sheet was completed by Jonathan Lotson April 17, 2018. I had originally called him and discussed the project at length. After that, I emailed the words to him and music of the song from 1926, keeping in mind the original words of the song that was written as "Come By Here," and then later was made famous by pronouncing the words "Kumbaya". So on April 13, 2018, Jonathan, a musical composer and writer, and I were successful in completing the first draft, April 17, 2018.

The words below are what I sent to Jonathan. As an accomplished composer, he translated the original music. Sent by email, this is the actual words below, from me to Jonathan:

Email from: Geechee Gullah Ring Shouters <geecheegullahringshouters@gmail.com>Date: February 13, 2018 at 11:36:52 PM EST

To: jlotson@yahoo.com, Griffin Lotson griffinlotson@gmail.com Subject: Sheet music by Jonathan Lotson, words by Griffin Lotson

OK Jonathan, this is the main thing you need to work on in our project. This is what we want to see below but in our name and our original sheet music and words. Take your time. Let us make history together. God bless our success for Gullah Geechee history, Georgia history, American history, and World history. This is the correct version, word for word to the original "Come by Ya" aka, "Come By Here", aka "Kumbaya"

Somebody need you Lord, come by Ya
Somebody need you Lord, come by Ya
Oh, Lord, come by Ya,
I need you Lord, come by Ya
Sinner need you Lord, come by Ya.
Sinner need you Lord, come by Ya, oh, Lord, come by Ya
Come by ya Lord, come by Ya
Come by ya my Lord, come by Ya,
Come by ya my Lord, come by Ya, oh, Lord, come by Ya
In the morn in, dear Lord, come by Ya, in the mornin,
"O" Lord, come by Ya,
In the morn in, dear Lord, come by Ya, oh, Lord, come by Ya,......
Oh, Lord, come by Ya,
Yonder need you Lord, come by Ya,
yonder need you Lord, come by Ya,
Yonder need you Lord, come by Ya, oh, Lord, come by Ya
Oh, sinner need you Lord, come by here,
Sinner need you Lord, come by here,
Sinner need you Lord, Come by here, oh my Lord,
won't you come by Ya,
In the morn in', morn in', won't you come by here,
morn in morn in, wan't you come by here,
in the morn in, morn in, want you come by here
Oh, Lord, come by here.

Griffin and Jonathan Lotson

Making history with the "Kumbaya" song and phase.

My nephew Jonathan Lotson in the photo above on the right* is a notable musician who graduated from the world famous Berkeley School of Music. Now he's helping make history with an old song, giving back to his culture of "Gullah Geechee". This represents the first Gullah Geechee translation in the world of the original words that were sung by the original singer, Henry Wylie (Wylly) of the now famous 1926 recording of "Kumbaya".

Come By Ya
Internationally Known as Kumbaya

Griffin Lotson translation of the original
Gullah Geechee words, as said by Sing
H. Wiley a.k.a. Henry Wylie (Wiley)

Transcribed by Jonathan Lotson
Original musical notes with voice notation 1926
H. Wiley a.k.a. Henry Wylie (Wiley) 1926

mor-nin dear Lord come by ya Oh Lord come by ya O - Oh Lord
come by ya Yon-der need you Lord come by ya Yon-der need you Lord
come by ya Yon-der need you Lord come by ya O - Oh Lord
come by ya Oh sin-ner need you Lord come by here Sin-ner need you Lord
come by here Sin-ner need you Lord come by here Oh my Lord wan't you
come by ya In the morn - nin morn - nin wan't you come by here
In the morn - nin wan't you morn - nin morn - in wan't you
come by here O - Oh Lord come by here

Kumbaya: Finding History

Chris Smith, a researcher in the AFC reading room, was working on an index of the Gordon recordings, and I found out more about Wylie, the singer that was recorded 1926 on the cylinder. Smith found that Wylie's recordings seem interspersed with those of Jeff Union, who was recorded on April 17, 1926, at W.T. Marlow's prison camp in Darien. Therefore, it is likely that Wylie's recordings were made at the same place. We do know if they were recorded on the same day, April 17, 1926, by each of them talking at the end of their recording.

Henry Wylly's draft card was founded by Chris Smith and Griffin Lotson. We believe this is the same man who sang "Come By Here" for Robert W. Gordon on April 17, 1926. Looking for draft and census information, Smith found documents which may give a few details of the singer's life. Smith writes:

"Henry Wylly, born September 26,1899, registered for the draft on September 12 1918, checking the box 'negro,' and making his mark rather than signing. He was a boat hand, living in Crescent, McIntosh County, Georgia. He is married to Felia (it looks like) Wylly, resident in Eulonia, which is also in McIntosh County. Henry Wylly also appears in the 1920 census as a 'mulatto,' widowed, aged 20, and a convict in the Darien county jail. Darien is the county seat of McIntosh County. It's not clear to me whether this is the same man as Henry A. Wiley, sentenced to life for murder in McIntosh County, received into the system on July 22, 1919: escaped on July 26, 1926. There's a tick, but no date, in the 'Recaptured' column of the register". I, Griffin Lotson, did some more research on this and received more fascinating information.

Various publications from the era of Wylie's performance suggest the song's range and its influence. In 1926, for example, a song entitled "Oh, Lordy Won't You Come By Here" was published by the songwriter Madelyn Sheppard, as described by weiter. Madelyn was later half of a songwriting duo with Annelu Burns. (Sheppard and Burns were notable for being two white women from Selma, Alabama, who composed blues songs and spirituals in African American dialect and sold them to African American publishers, including W.C. Handy. Sheppard's song is not the same song as "Kumbaya," but its publication in the era during which the earliest versions of "Kumbaya" were emerging suggests that she was familiar with the traditional song. In 1931, the Society for the Preservation of Spirituals published a song that they called "Come by Yuh," in a book entitled The Carolina Low Country. The exact date of the song's collection is not mentioned in the book, but all of the book's songs were collected between 1922 and 1931. (As a consequence, it is impossible to know whether this version predates any or all of Gordon's materials, and it, therefore may be impossible to identify with certainty the first verifiable reference to the song).

This song has the refrain "come by yuh, Lord, come by yuh," (Come By Ya) and a repeated verse "somebody need you Lord, come by yuh." Gordon called one of his now-unplayable cylinders "Come by here, Lord, come by here," and the other "Somebody need you Lord, come by here," suggesting that these were all the same song. It is also very similar to the song we know as "Kumbaya." By 1931, then, the song had likely been recorded or transcribed from at least five singers, and other songs bearing the stamp of its influence had been recorded and published as well.

In 1936, John Lomax, Gordon's successor as head of the Archive, recorded another version of "Come by Here" for the archive. The singer was Ethel Best of Raiford, Florida. Each verse was a single line repeated 3 times, followed by "oh, Lord, come by here."

(1) Come by here, my lord, come by here
(2) Well we [down in?) trouble, Lord, come by here
(3) Well, it's somebody needs you lord, come by here
(4) Come by here, my lord, come by here
(5) Well it's somebody sick Lord come by here
(6) Well, we need you Jesus Lord to come by here
(7) Come by here, my Lord, come by here
(8) Somebody moanin', Lord, come by here

Come by Here. Sung by Ethel Best in Raiford, Florida, 1936: recorded by John A. Lomax, This song came to be known as 'Kumbaya.' The chorus singing with Best is unidentified. In the late 1930s and early 1940s, the archive recorded the song several more times in Mississippi, Alabama, and Texas. Pete Seeger made one of the earliest popular recordings of the song "Kumbaya."

New Evidence of the Song's Early History

Clearly, by the advent of the 1940s, "Come By Here" was a widely known spiritual among African Americans in the South. Yet, as noted above, the song has often been identified as a 1936 composition of New York City songwriter and evangelist Marvin V. Frey (1918-1992). As we have seen, this confusion stems from claims made by Frey himself; in 1939, Frey published a version entitled "Come By Here," on which he claimed copyright. Frey claimed to have written the words in 1936, based on a prayer he had heard from an evangelist in Oregon. Frey might have been basing his story on the truth; the evangelist he mentions could have been adapting the song, which, as we have seen, was already widely known by then. To what extent, then, was his "Come By Here" an original composition?

Chee-Hoo Lum attempted to answer this question in his article written 2006-2017. Unfortunately, by skipping over the 1926 Georgia performance by H. Wylie (recorded by Gordon) to present the 1936 Florida performance by Ethel Best (recorded by Lomax); Lum missed the opportunity to compare Frey's song with Wylie's, or with popular versions of "Kumbaya." He seems to find the 1931 publication in South Carolina Low Country to be insufficiently close to Frey's later version to constitute clear evidence that Frey's composition was based on the traditional song. Therefore, he concludes that Frey's authorship claim is "the first possible 'origin' theory" for the song. Wylie's version, however, preserved by AFC on a cylinder recording, is closer to Frey's, in both lyrics and music, and predates it by almost ten years. Given the existence of Wylie's version, then, Frey's claim to have composed the song based on a spoken prayer, rather than a song, becomes very unlikely.

Moreover, the plausibility of Frey's claim to have written the song also depended on another factor: Frey was obligated to explain how a song written by a white man and called "Come By Here," had become "Kum Ba Yah" or "Kumbaya" in the oral tradition. After all, a song written in standard English, and originally disseminated in print as "Come By Here," would be more likely to enter oral tradition in Standard English, and to be collected with a pronunciation closer to that dialect. One of Frey's stories about the song had the effect of explaining this anomaly; he told it to Peter Blood-Patterson, who sent it to the AFC archive in 1993. It is filed in the "Kum Ba Yah" subject file:

According to Frey the pronunciation "Kum Ba Yah", also spelled "Kumbaya" originated when Luvale-speaking people in Angola and Zaire translated "Come by Here" into their language. That strains credibility on several levels, primarily that "Come by Here" translated into Luvale would not be "Kum Ba Yah". Indeed, for "Come by Here" to translate to "Kum Ba Yah," the target language would have to be Creole with English as one of its main components. No such language was common in Angola (then still a Portuguese colony) or Zaire (a country formerly colonized by Belgium, whose primary colonial language was French) in the 1930s. Moreover, the AFC's cylinder recording of H. Wylie shows that we have no need of such a story. In Wylie's dialect, which is Gullah Geechee, the word "here" is pronounced as "Ya," rendering the song's most repeated line "come by ya," a phrase that can be phonetically rendered as either "Kum Ba Yah" or "Kumbaya."

A marker near Marvin V. Frey's grave site in the West Barre Cemetery in Orleans County, New York, which still advances his claim to the authorship of "Kum Ba Yah." If Frey's claim to have composed the song becomes more farfetched in light of this cylinder recording, so does the notion that the song originated in Africa. The idea of an African origin was based on the understanding of Lynn and Katherine Rohrbough, who published song books through the Cooperative Recreation Service of Delaware, Ohio. (AFC has acquired their collection, a major resource for the study of folk songs in schools and summer camps.)

As the Folksmiths' liner notes explain, the Rohrboughs heard the song from an Ohio professor, who claimed to have heard it from a missionary in Africa. No account that I have seen establishes a date for this occurrence, so the idea that the song was African in origin (rather than an American song that had traveled to Africa) seems to have been based on the fact that the words "Kum Ba Ya" sounded vaguely African, and the fact that the Rohrboughs were unaware of American versions that predated their own publications of the song. Indeed, according to Frey's interview with Blood- Patterson, once the Rohrboughs learned of Frey's previous claim, they conceded that the song was Frey's, so they seem to have had little confidence in their own claim of an African origin for the song. Thus, AFC's cylinder, with a pronunciation very close to "Kum Ba Yah," would seem to eliminate the last piece of circumstantial evidence for an African origin.

The Folksmiths, in 1957, made the first folk revival recording of "Kumbaya."

Finally, according to Stephen Winick research and article, the theory about the song (that it originated in Gullah Geechee) is still possible, but it's weakened by the Boyd manuscript. Even without that version, it is clear from AFC recordings that "Come by Here" was known fairly early throughout the

American South, including Texas, Alabama, Florida, and Mississippi. Before the rediscovery of the Boyd manuscript, however, the first known versions were Gordon's cylinders, which were from Georgia, and the transcription published in The Carolina Low Country, which was from South Carolina.

These are all most likely Gullah versions. Their appearance so early in the song's history suggested to most scholars that the song originated in the Gullah Geechee region and spread from there. The Boyd manuscript, however, is from Alliance, North Carolina, significantly north of Gullah territory. However, because of new research we can now show there were enslave plantations in the same county of the city of Alliance North Carolina/ Pamlico County, N.C. In fact the Gullah Geechee Cultural Heritage area extends to North Carolina, but this may not have been known to the Library of Congress in 2010. ("John N. Benners' Journal: A Saltwater Farmer & His Slaves").

Therefore, from the time of the song's earliest record, it seems to have been shared among both Gullah speakers and speakers of other African-American dialects. Given this, although a Gullah Geechee origin is certainly still possible, I, Griffin Lotson can be fully confident that the song originated in Gullah Geechee dialect, rather than in African American English more generally. It is certainly likely that Gullah Geechee versions led to it becoming a popular song today.

Words from Stephen Winick and Griffin Lotson "In summary, the evidence from the American Folklife Center Archive does suggests that "Kumbaya" is an African American spiritual which originated somewhere in the American South (Gullah Geechee), and then traveled all over the world: to Africa, where missionaries sang it for new converts; to the northwestern United States, to Coastal Georgia and South Carolina, where it was adapted into the Gullah dialect. It was likely versions in Gullah Geechee dialect that made it into "Kumbaya" and into the Northeastern United States, where it entered the repertoires of such singers as Pete Seeger and Joan Baez, and eventually to Europe, South America, Australia, and other parts of the world, where revival recordings of the song abound. Although it is truly a global folk song, its earliest versions are preserved in only one place: the AFC Archive".

The adoption of the song "Kumbaya" into the folk revival also has connections with the American Folklife Center Archive. As we have already seen, the song became popular after it was published by Lynn and Katherine Rohrbough. In 1957, folksinger Tony Saletan learned the song from the Rohrboughs. He taught it to a group from Oberlin College known as The Folksmiths. The Folksmiths toured summer camps in the summer of 1957, and they taught "Kumbaya" (or, as they called it, "Kum Ba Yah") to thousands of American campers, helping to cement the song's association with both children and campfires. The Folksmiths also recorded the song in August, 1957, on an album called "We've Got Some Singing to Do", which was released on the Folkways label in early 1958. This was the first published recording of the song. Later that same year, Folkways released a version by Pete Seeger, with the title "Kumbaya." In 1959, Seeger's group, The Weavers recorded the song, this time as "Kumbaya." The transformation of the song's title from "Come by Here/Come by Yah" to "Kumbaya" was complete.

Later folk revival versions of the song undoubtedly derive from these three influential recordings, all of which have connections to AFC's Archive. Seeger was an intern at the Archive in the 1930s, and has revisited AFC many times since then, most recently in 2007. In several recent interviews, he has made it clear that he once heard the extant Gordon cylinder recording of "Come by Here" at the Archive, although he is not sure when this visit to the Archive occurred. As for Hickerson, after his one year with the Folksmiths, he trained as a folklorist and archivist and got a job at the AFC Archive; he eventually rose to be head of the Archive, a position from which he retired in 1998. The moral of the story seems to be: while you can take "Kumbaya" out of the AFC Archive, you can't take the Archive out of "Kumbaya".

After reading an article that was placed on the Internet from one of the authors and writings of the Library of Congress that mentioned my name, Griffin Lotson, it was exhilarating. I felt privileged that I played a part in history. I thought I'd be the first to complement them on their efforts of agreeing with some of our efforts to help further the history of the world's most popular song or maybe I should say one of the world's most popular songs with over one billion individuals knowing about this song or at least the phrase, all over the world, I would venture to say on every continent on the planet earth.

Who would've ever thought the first known recording would be made in the small town of Darien in McIntosh County, Georgia. As I often say, everything has to be from somewhere, so why not from the city of Darien, Georgia. As I may have said earlier in this book, some contents are written just for historic significance. In this part of this book, here is my very special tribute to the Library of Congress writer Stephen Winick, PhD historian.

Kumbaya: Email

Recent Trip to Germany researching worldwide history of Kumbaya, the book in the tope photo name: Die Mundorgel (The Mouth Organ) persons in the photo below: Left Mr. Klaus Kramer, Griffin Lotson Carlinda N. Lotson (Daughter of the author) and Mrs. Cornelia Kramer.

Kumbaya: Email

Griffin Lotson

February 7, 2018 at 1:07 am, by email

A very special thank you to top executives from the Library of Congress, namely, Todd Harvey and Elizabeth Peterson, for providing me the opportunity to continue my recent discovery and research on the history of the Kumbaya song, now having its rightful place in history.

For nearly six consecutive years I have been finding new information about the song "Kumbaya" gladly working with these outstanding individuals from the Library of Congress, state legislators, and Federal Government congressional officials, as well as many others. (A true good "Kumbaya" moment of all working together for the good).

I was born into the Gullah Geechee culture. I truly do give a special thanks to a lady by the name of Sudy Leavy who first asked me to look into the research 2011- 2012, with a special thank you to the Library of Congress for allowing me to work with each of you over the last several years in the Folklife Center of America. Now we have over one billion people in the world that know this song or the phrase "Kumbaya" aka "Come By Ya".

The original first known recording in the world was made in 1926, sung by Henry Wylie (Henry Wiley) of the Gullah Geechee African-American culture from Darien, Georgia and recorded by Robert Winslow Gordon. Thanks to each of you.

The American Folklife Center was created by the United States Congress in 1976 to "preserve and present American Folklife," but its roots can be traced to the establishment of the Archive of American Folk Song in the Library's Music Division in 1928. That year, the Library of Congress, Herbert Putnam (1861-1955), invited Robert Winslow Gordon (1888-1961) to become a "specialist and consultant in the field of folk song and literature." Gordon was already a devoted collector of American folk music: as a Harvard student between 1906 and 1917, he conceived of a "national project" to collect the entire body of American folk music.

Leaving graduate school to pursue his dream, he traveled extensively throughout the United States recording folk songs with an Edison wax-cylinder machine, supporting himself through teaching, writing, and the occasional grant. He convinced Carl Engel, the chief of the Library of Congress's Music Division, that grassroots traditions should be represented at the national library. Through his efforts, the Archive of American Folksong was established with private funding, and Gordon was appointed its director. (For more about Gordon and examples from his collections, see the online presentation: Folk-Songs of America: The Robert Winslow Gordon Collection, 1922-1932).

Robert Winslow Gordon, the first Head of the Archive of American Folk-Song. 1928.

First head of the Archive of Folk Song, Robert W. Gordon is shown in a photo in the southwest attic of the Library of Congress building, Washington, DC in 1930.

Unfortunately, Gordon's position at the Library eventually ended when funding faltered. However, the idea of a national folk archive had taken root, and it was revived when the Texan folk song collector John A. Lomax (1867-1948) came to the Library in 1933. John was assisted by his young son Alan Lomax (1915-2002), who in 1936 became the Archive's first federally funded staff member. In 1937, Alan was promoted to "assistant in charge".

On behalf of the Library, the younger Lomax undertook important collecting expeditions throughout the eastern United States; produced a seminal series of documentary folk music albums entitled "Folk Music of the United States," and recorded legendary performers including jazz musician Jelly Roll Morton and folk singers Lead Belly (Huddie William Ledbetter) and Woody Guthrie. In the years that followed, Alan introduced audiences in Washington, D.C., and radio audiences throughout the United States, to the richness of America's traditional music and musicians. The thoughts for this section of the book are purely for history and historical accuracy. So often we see so much of history was and is lost because someone or some group did not take the time to write or remember the past by telling it to others, recording or filming to pass it on to the next generation. We did not need to let this history go away without others knowing the true history of 1950s "Kumbaya" AKA 1930s "Come By Here" and the not so famous words but the first un-know words 1926: "Come By Ya". My first thoughts of researching this song were not my own. It was presented to me by a dear friend, Ms. Sudy Leavy. The year was 2011. Ms. Sudy had approached me about some research she had been working on at the Library of Congress in Washington, D.C. At the time, both of us were living in the city of Darien, Georgia. Fortunately and surprisingly, Ms. Sudy had travel to see our group in Washington, D.C. the "Geechee Gullah Ring Shouters". We had a presentation to do for the Smithsonian at the Anacostia Community Museum, on linguist Lorenzo Dow Turner.

This was an exhibit that dealt with Gullah Geechee history. It was a very exciting trip. Very surprisingly, our group from a very small city called Darien was doing something that had never been done before. Not only did we set the Guinness Book of World Records for the largest Ring Shout in the world, it was the largest gathering of Gullah Geechee's at the U.S. Capital and largest gathering at any given time for visitation of Gullah Geechee's ever to visit the White House in Washington, D.C. It was a very special time in the month of July, 2011. Individuals traveled from all over the United States to make history.

New Harmonies: Celebrating American Roots Music

After the Washington, D.C. trip, my friend Sudy, and I connected in Darien to start working on another very special project that she wanted me to be a part of, called "New Harmony". Neither of us knew that it was going to lead us to new "Kumbaya" history.

The New Harmony project was a series of exhibits traveling throughout small town America, highlighting the music and individuals that made America great and some of the most popular well- known and not so well-known artists that contributed to music, presented by the Georgia Humanities Council in Darien.

Sudy Leavy and Griffin Lotson (Grandson in background) 2012

The local coordinators for the exhibit were author and historian Sudy Leavy and Michele Nicole Johnson, manager of Hog Hammock Public Library on Sapelo Island, just offshore from mainland McIntosh County. I was invited as well as many other individuals and organizations to a special presentation on the project, and we all were told that Darien had been chosen as one of 12 Georgia towns that would host New Harmonies: Celebrating American Roots Music, a traveling exhibit from the Smithsonian Institution in Washington, D.C. The New Harmonies exhibit would be in Darien from July 21, 2012 through Sept. 1, 2012.

The exhibit was also to celebrate and add our local musical and individual history to accompany the New Harmonies' musical history exhibit. Sudy and Michele were looking for volunteers to serve on an advisory committee as well as organizations interested in hosting music related programs and exhibits. The presentation was on Wednesday, August 3, 2011 at the Ida Hilton Public Library in Darien.

New Harmonies took a look back at "roots music" and how it has served as the foundation for blues, country, gospel, rhythm and blues, folk and rock and roll, and many other musical genres appreciated worldwide today.

The musical history of Darien and its surrounding coastal communities wraps itself around telling stories through song, from echoes of Indian drums, African rhythms, and Scottish bagpipes, to today's most popular beats. Folklorists Lydia Parrish and Robert Winslow Gordon captured the rowing songs, work songs, reels, rags, shanties, and shouts of African Americans in the 1920s and '30s. While visiting the Georgia coast in the 1930s, linguist Lorenzo Dow Turner recorded many songs, among them a Mende funeral song, "Awaka" that had survived the treacherous Middle Passage. Legendary recording artists -- including James Brown, Otis Redding, and the Temptations, to name a few -- performed here at a club called Jake's in Darien as part of the "Chitlin' Circuit" from the 1940s through the '70s.

How did I come up with the idea to make all this new discovery, research, and findings happen? First we needed the State of Georgia to give historical recognition, this was not easy, then the next step maybe National and International, maybe impossible, but we had to try.

Georgia' First Official Historic Song, "Kumbaya"

For historical purposes, I'd like to go into detail. Perhaps it's not necessary, but I found out quite a bit with history that has been left out when it comes to details. I don't want to repeat history and leave out these finite details that might be important for future records, because I believe it will be important not only for now but also in the future.

From the beginning, it was about August 2011, shortly after I came back from the trip to Washington, D.C. with the Geechee Gullah Ring Shouters. I was serving as the manager of the group. We, together with others made history by setting the Guinness Book of World Records by participating in the Lorenzo D. Turner exhibit at the Anacostia Community Museum, in Washington, D.C. Others had traveled from Georgia including Ms. Sudy Leavy and many others from around the United States.

Once we were back in Darien, Ms. Leavy approached me with some papers she had received from the Library of Congress. If my memory serves me, I believe her first question was did I know anything about some recordings concerning the Lotsons at the Library of Congress, in Washington? My reply to her was "no"; I didn't know of any significant things that were at the Library of Congress concerning my surname Lotson. Of course, that really did peak my interest at the time. As she handed the papers to me that showed the Lotsons' name, she also asked me about some other recordings that she thought maybe, might be of significance. One of those recordings was the song "Come By Here" as it was written on the Library of Congress paper. For historical record purposes, that was exciting. Maybe there was a possibility that the "Come By Here" song could maybe, might, have something to do with the very famous song "Kumbaya".

But to be honest, I was more excited at the moment about finding out about the Lotson's name. Of course that came natural, because my name is Griffin "Lotson" and of course my father is a "Lotson" and grandfather and from there, down through history the name Lotson goes back on my father's side of my family, going back to the early 1800s. (My mother's surname was Sams and her father's name was Nelson Sams. My grandfather, as well as my beloved uncle's name on my mother's side of the family was Isaac Sams, all of whom I knew very well).

All the hard work has finally paid off, from doing interviews from around the world with media such as the New York Times, BBC world news, television, video, college, universities, and movie productions. The next two documents below will give testament to local, state, American, and world history. This gives prudence and serendipity that one person of Gullah Geechee descendants that came from enslavement in America, can do additional research that could bring the truth out for all to know, now it's my hope that everyone who reads this book will take some time beyond yourself and document the history that is so significant to you and others.

My dear friend Sudy also mentioned very important names of individuals in songs she hoped I would perhaps look into or research. It is good to know that in life it's very exhilarating to know you have done something that's beyond yourself, something that will change the course of history, something so significant that it's worth giving up your time, your energy, your efforts, your money; your rest. It is an underlying experience to know that I have done such a thing in researching this internationally known song "Kumbaya" and "Phrase".

The State of Georgia's First State Historical Song in nearly 300 years

Regular Session - SR 293
"Kumbaya"; recognize Georgia's first state historical song.

Feb/23/2017 - Senate Read and Adopted: Senate Resolution 293

By: Senators Ligon, Jr. of the 3rd, Watson of the 1st, Jackson of the 2nd, Hill of the 4th, Cowsert of the 46th, and others

A RESOLUTION

1 Recognizing Georgia's first state historical
song, known worldwide as "Kumbaya" and for
2 other purposes.
3 WHEREAS, the Library of Congress has
documented American folk songs throughout the
4 nation's history, and
5 WHEREAS, the first director of the Archive of American Folk-Song at the Library of
6 Congress, Robert Winslow Gordon, pioneered early efforts to record folk songs by
7 transporting his heavy wax cylinder recorder

by rail, car, horse, and boat to remote regions
8 of the nation; and
9 WHEREAS, Mr. Gordon traveled to Darien and
the Sea Islands of Georgia in 1926 to record
10 numerous folk songs in the Gullah Dialect,
also known as the Sea Islands Creole Dialect, and
11 WHEREAS, Mr. H. Wylie, an African American of Gullah Geechee
heritage, gave
12 permission for him to record the spiritual folk song "Come by Here", and
13 WHEREAS, the Library of Congress states
that this is the first known recording of "Come
14 by Here," a song that came to be known as "Kumbaya", and
15 WHEREAS, "Kumbaya," first recorded in Georgia, has become a song
with national
16 significance in American culture.
17 NOW, THEREFORE, BE IT RESOLVED BY
THE SENATE that the members of this body
18 recognize this historical song of Georgia
and its significance to our state and to the
19 Gullah Geechee culture.

National Recognition United States Congress Washington, D.C. at the U.S. Capital

December 7, 2017, as read at the United States Capital in Washington, D.C. by U S Congressman Buddy Carter from the State of Georgia's First Congressional District:

Mr. CARTER of Georgia. Mr. Speaker, I rise today to recognize a very important song to the history of the State of Georgia, "Kumbaya".

The first known recording of "Kumbaya" took place in 1926 near Darien, Georgia. The original name was "Come By Here," but now the song is internationally known as "Kumbaya." For the serious minded historian or researcher, you'll be able to find this in the Congressional Records for the world to follow, see, and know:

Congressional Record Volume 163, Number 200 (Thursday, December 7, 2017)]

[Pages H9714-H9715]

While the exact origin of the song is uncertain, scholars believe it originated with the Gullah Geechee people, who are descendants of enslaved African Americans who lived on the Sea Islands in the coastal regions of Georgia.

It is largely believed that the song was a plea for God's intervention for this group of African Americans, asking Him to relieve them from a number of different hard times in the community: a sick family member, oppression, and more.

Robert Winslow Gordon, a staff member and eventually founder of the Library of Congress' Archives of Folk Song, was temporarily living in Georgia in 1926 and took the first recording of "Kumbaya" on a wax cylinder recorder numbered A839, still located in the Library of Congress today. He recorded a person in the Gullah Geechee community named H. Wylie, who sang the lyrics: "need you Lord, come by here. Somebody need you, Lord, come by here " .This recording of "Kumbaya" is one of the earliest items located in the Library of Congress' Archive of Folk Song. Today, Robert Winslow Gordon is buried in Darien, Georgia, home of that first recording of "Kumbaya".

Scholars think that "come by here" simply sounded like "Kumbaya" to some listeners, a nonexistent word at the time that evolved into the song that we have here today. Other scholars think that the original song was not even "come by here," but instead "come by ya."

Since that time, the song has spread throughout our Nation and the world. Recordings can even be found sung by Americans throughout all different times in our Nation's history.

There are 1930s recordings from central Texas and in Florida, while many Americans were finding solace during the Jim Crow period. In the 1950s and 1960s, "Kumbaya" was sung by Pete Seeger; Peter, Paul, and Mary, and Joan Baez. The song has even been traced to Angola, transported by missionaries.

Even today, "Kumbaya" means something different to different groups of people, but we should never forget the original meaning of the song and who we believe may be the original creators of the song, the Gullah Geechee people.

The Gullah Geechee people live on the southeastern coast, from St. Augustine, Florida, up through Georgia, and South Carolina, to their northernmost area of Wilmington, North Carolina. Most of these areas refer to the people as Gullah, but in Georgia, we call them Geechee. They are the direct descendants of enslaved Americans who arrived here from west and central Africa to produce rice for slave holding Americans.

There are many aspects of their culture that are unique, complex, and beautiful. Their language is based in Creole and is the only distinctly African Creole language in the United States. The Gullah Geechee people make sweetgrass baskets designed for rice production as a craft passed down to both men and women.

Although this culture and their traditions have modernized since the 19th century and early 20th century in America, today you can still see the Gullah Geechee people weaving sweetgrass baskets and living their culture in other ways if you drive through coastal Georgia.

I cannot overstate the importance this group of people has had on the development and history of the First Congressional District of Georgia, and I want to thank them for their contributions to this area.

Further, as creators of the song "Kumbaya," they have changed lives and have been a significant force not only in the First Congressional District of Georgia, but across the world and throughout American history. To recognize just how widespread this song has become, the Georgia General Assembly passed a resolution officially stating the impact this song has had on our State.

I hope you all will join me in our Nation's Capital by also recognizing the importance of this song. I am very proud that it originated in the First Congressional District of Georgia, a district that I have the honor and privilege of representing. It is also an honor to have members of the Gullah Geechee community from my district here at the Capitol today.

Welcome to our Nation's Capital. Thank you for your contribution to our Nation's history.

December 7, 2017.

News from U. S. Congressman Buddy Carter

Thursday, December 7, 2017

Every day is a special day at the Capitol but when we have visitors from back home, it is even more special. Today is one of those even more special days as we have representatives from the Gullah Geechee Cultural Heritage Commission and leaders from Darien and McIntosh County join us. Darien Mayor Bubba Hodge, Mayor Pro Tem Griffin Lotson, Darien News publisher Kathleen Russell and others are joined by curators from the American Folklife Center at the Library of Congress as we are celebrating the origin of the American song "Kumbaya." After meeting in my office, we all head down to the House Chamber where the group observes in the balcony and I have the honor of recognizing this special occasion during the morning session.

The Team That Changed History

Far left, Tim Sweezey (City of Darien manager), Heather Hodges (Executive Director, National Gullah Geechee Culture Heritage Commission), Todd Harvey (Executive at the Library of Congress), Mandy Harrison (Executive Director, Darien, McIntosh County, Chamber of Commerce), Elizabeth "Betsy" Peterson (National Director of the American Folklife Center, at the Library of Congress), Augustus Skeen, (City Councilman), Richard Braun (Darien City Attorney), Kathleen Russell, Publisher and Editor, Darien News), front row, Griffin Lotson, (Mayor Pro Tem), Buddy Carter (U. S. Congressman), Hugh " Bubba" Hodge (Mayor Of Darien), Barbara Shaw (Councilman).

New York Times

About That Song You've Heard, Kumbaya

By John Eligon. Feb. 9, 2018 New York Times

We chant it with locked arms and closed eyes, at campfires, in protest lines and from the pews at church, but the truth is, many of us have no clue what the lyrics mean or exactly where they come from.

Kumbaya my Lord, Kumbaya. Kumbaya my Lord, Kumbaya.

Thanks to research and lobbying by residents of a coastal community descended from slaves, the origins and meaning of "Kumbaya" have been recognized in Congress, raising hopes that a fading culture might get a boost. The song may be sung more often than usual this month, especially in the part of Georgia where its soulful lyrics are said to have originated almost a century ago. Speaking on the House floor two months back, Representative Buddy Carter of Georgia recognized the Gullah Geechee, whose ancestors were brought to America's southeastern coast from West Africa, as the probable creators of the famous folk song.

If you're searching for deep meaning in the word itself, the truth, as Mr. Carter laid out in his proclamation, is that "Kumbaya" is probably a made-up word. Still, it has come to evoke peace and harmony — sometimes mockingly so. The first known recording of the song was made in Darien, Ga., in 1926, sung by a Gullah Geechee man named H. Wylie. The chorus was actually "Come By Here," which in the Gullah's Creole accent sounds like cum-by-yah. Over time, that pronunciation transformed into what we know today as "Kumbaya". The hymn was a call to God to come and help the people as they faced oppression.

The Gullah Geechee, who have seen their land and way of life threatened by rising property values, now hope to use the Congressional proclamation, as well as the Georgia legislature's recognition of "Kumbaya" as the state's historical song, to help promote their story. An exhibition about the song is planned for this month in Darien, which sits along the 1,200-mile coastal corridor where the Gullah people settled.

"It's significant," said Anne C. Bailey, a historian at Binghamton University and author of "The Weeping Time," a book about the largest slave auction in America. "It says something about the African-American tradition and the African-American contribution to the building up of the country and the world."

Someone's singing Lord, Kumbaya. Someone's singing Lord, Kumbaya.

For decades, the dominant narrative was that of a white evangelist, the Rev. Marvin V. Frey, had originally composed "Kumbaya." This story was spread in part by Mr. Frey himself, who got a copyright on the song in 1939, claiming to have written it in 1936 based on a prayer he heard in Oregon. Something about that story never sat right with Stephen Winick, who has a PhD. D. in folklore. For one, the song sounds like something from the African-American tradition. Mr. Winick had also heard rumors that there was an earlier recording of the song in the archives of the American Folklife Center at the Library of Congress, where he works.

"I think it's important to restore cultural materials to their communities of origin," he said. "Give credit where it's due." Several years ago, Mr. Winick dug up that old wax cylinder recording. It was captured in 1926 by Robert Winslow Gordon, the first head of the Archive of American Folk Song. It was the recording of H. Wylie singing "Come By Here" in an accent that sounds like "Kumbaya," a decade before Mr. Frey claimed to have written "Kumbaya." Mr. Winick said it was possible that Mr. Frey may have heard a prayer with the "Kumbaya" lyrics, and composed them into a song, thinking he was the first to do so. But the evidence on that remains murky. Mr. Winick also found in the archives lyrics collected in 1926 by a high school student outside of Gullah territory for a song similar to "Come By Here." That raised the possibility, Mr. Winick said, that the song might not have originated with the Gullah Geechee, though he maintains that it is quite possible that they could be its creators. The version of the song as we know it today very likely traces to the Gullahs because of the pronunciation of "come by here" as "Kumbaya," he said. "I think that in the general public, if you ask someone on the street, 'What does "Kumbaya" mean,' they wouldn't know," he said. "They would think it means joining hands and being friendly to each other."

Someone's laughing, Lord, kumbaya. Someone's laughing, Lord, kumbaya.

Griffin Lotson, the Gullah historian, knew nothing of the song's connection to his people until he started researching it in 2012, and since then he has been on something of a crusade to elevate its history. Many Gullah Geechee's, Mr. Lotson included, were conditioned to think that in order to live a successful life, they had to leave their dialect and traditions behind, he said. But now there is great interest in Gullah culture, from inside and out.

He was hired to consult on a scene in the remake of the television mini-series "Roots." He is often called upon to give cultural tours. Lawmakers realized the importance of preserving the Gullah Geechee culture years ago when, in 2006, Congress created the Gullah Geechee Cultural Heritage Corridor. The Gullah Geechee's hope that the recognition of their role in the origins of "Kumbaya" will represent one step toward popularizing, and preserving, who they are.

"Gullah Geechee culture has influenced everything, from our music to the way we speak," Heather Lorraine Hodges, the executive director of the Gullah Geechee Cultural Heritage Corridor Commission, wrote in an email. "It is a foundational culture for the United States."

Someone's crying, Lord, kumbaya. Someone's crying, Lord, kumbaya.

More emails for historical significance and for archival records are available for years and centuries to come, See the 21st-century communication via email from researchers Chris Smith, Todd Harvey, Stephen Winick and myself.

September 25, 2018: Email from Griffin Lotson

Hi Nicole and Todd, this is Griffin Lotson one more time. I need your help to get Chris Smith, a researcher in the AFC reading room and is working on an index of the Gordon recordings. I need his email and or phone number, please.

According to Stephen Winick, the writer of the 2010 article on Kumbaya from the Library of Congress, Chris Smith has found out more about Wylie, the singer who recorded on the cylinder. Smith found that Wylie's recordings seem interspersed with those of Jeff Union, who was recorded on April 17, 1926, at W.T. Marlow's prison camp in Darien. Therefore, it is likely that Wylie' recordings were made at the same place. (My research shows little difference.., we know now they both were recorded the same day in Darien, and maybe they both were recorded when Jeff and Wylie were in jail/prison camp in Darien April 1, 1926).

Maybe with Mr. Chris Smith and I, Griffin Lotson, conferring with each other and sharing notes, we may be able to clear up some of the mysteries of the song "Kumbaya". Yes, I had the fascinating opportunity to go to the Virginia campus of recordings of the Library of Congress, and to actually hold the original 1926 cylinder and to listen to some of the history that was hidden for nearly a century now. Thanks for your help.

****

From: Griffin Lotson <griffinlotson@gmail.com>

Date: Wednesday, 26 September 2018 15:16

To: Todd Harvey

Cc: Chris Smith

Subject: Re: Question

Thanks Todd, I will look to getting an email or call from Chris Smith, the researcher in the AFC reading room. According to Stephen Winick, the writer of the 2010 article on Kumbaya from the Library of Congress, Chris Smith has found out more about Wylie, the singer recorded on the cylinder. Smith found that Wylie's recordings seem interspersed with those of Jeff Union, who was recorded on April 17, 1926, at W.T. Marlow's camp in Darien. Therefore, it is likely that Wylie's recordings were made at the same place. (My research shows little difference).

We know now they both were recorded the same day in Darien, and maybe they both were recorded when Jeff and Wylie were in jail/prison camp in Darien April 27, 1926?) Maybe with Mr. Chris Smith and I conferring with each other and sharing notes, we maybe can clear up some of the mysteries of the song "Kumbaya". Yes, I had the fantastic opportunity to go to the Virginia campus of recordings Library of Congress, and to actually hold the original 1926 cylinder and to listen to some of the history that was hidden for nearly a century now. Thanks for your help.

On Sep 26, 2018, at 4:08 PM, Chris Smith wrote: Hello Griffin I've received your message, and I'm happy to help, but right now it's late at night here in Britain, and I'm traveling to Italy tomorrow. I will try to make time to review my files and send you what I have on, Friday evening.

Best Wishes, Chris Smith

****

September 26, 2018 from Griffin Lotson to Chris 5:22 PM

Thanks Chris, and enjoy your travels. Thanks Griffin Lotson!!!

****

From Chris Smith to Griffin Lotson: September 28, 2018 around 3:10PM Eastern standard time:

Dear Griffin

Below is the part of my list of Robert Winslow Gordon recordings that includes Henry Wylie. He is only H. Wylie on the file card, but he announces his name, and the location (Darien) and the date, on the cylinder. You can see from the order of the song numbers (A prefix) and cylinder numbers (GA prefix) why I think he was a member of the work gang that Captain Marlow had — I assume — leased from the penitentiary.

JEFF UNION

Jeff Union, v.

Capt. W.T. Marlow's Camp, Darien, Ga.   Saturday, 17 April 1926

A-387 (GA-154)   Plumb De Line   LC

A-388 (GA-155)   The World Can't Do Me No Harm   LC

H. WYLIE Henry Wylie, v. Darien, Ga.   Saturday, 17 April 1926

A-389 (GA-156)   Come By Here   LC

The singer announces the location of cylinder 389 as Darien; it seems likely to have been recorded at Capt. W.T. Marlow's Camp, as were cylinders 387, 388, and 390 by Jeff Union, and 391 by an unidentified group.

JEFF UNION

Jeff Union, v.

Capt. W.T. Marlow's Camp, Darien, Ga.   Saturday, 17 April 1926

A-390 (GA-157)   I Told Jesus I'd Make Him A Soldier   LC

Unidentified Group, v.

Capt. W.T. Marlow's Camp, Darien area, Ga.   Saturday, 17 April 1926

A-391 (GA-158)   In The Bright Shining World   LC

H. WYLIE Henry Wylie, v. Darien area, Ga.   prob. late May 1926

[?] (GA-352)   Seaboard Air Line LC

And again, below is what I wrote to Stephen Winnick and Jennifer Cutting in 2016, with some new material:

Henry Wylly [sic], Negro, born September 26 1899, registered for the draft on September 12 1918, making his mark rather than signing. He was a boat hand, living in Crescent, McIntosh County. He was married to Felia (it looks like) Wylly's resident was in Eulonia, [McIntosh County.]

Henry Wylly [sic] appears in the 1920 census as a mulatto, widowed, aged 20, and a convict in the Darien county jail. Darien is the county seat of McIntosh County, of course.

It's not clear to me whether this is the same man as Henry A. Wiley [sic], sentenced to life for murder in McIntosh County; received into the system on July 22, 1919, and escaped on July 26, 1926. There's a tick, but no date, in the 'Recaptured' column of the register.

Note in 2018: I'm now sure – and I don't know why I was uncertain! – that this is the same man in all cases. He was married in 1918, sentenced to life for murder in 1919, and a widower in 1920. It's clear, I think, that he killed his wife. Also new in 2018: Wylie's unfortunate wife seems to have been the daughter of Charles and Janie Williams. She was enumerated in McIntosh County in 1900 as Felina Williams, born February 1896, and in 1910 as Fillier Williams, 13. Trying to track W.T. Marlow down, I've found marriages conducted in McIntosh and Glynn Counties around the turn of the 20th century by a W.T. Marlow, MG, which seems to stand for 'Minister of the Gospel'. If it's the same man, he seems to have moved on to being in charge of convict labor (presumably a chain gang) by 1926.

Jeff Union, recorded the same day, shows up only in the Georgia death index, born about 1891, died 6 January 1952 in McIntosh County. No image available on ancestry.com.

I hope this helps with your research. I'm copying it to Stephen and Jennifer, so that they are aware of the additional information. Attached is a file of documents on Henry and his wife. Best Wishes, Chris Smith.

September 28, 2018 time 3:32 PM From: Chris to Griffin

Here he is in the 1910 census, in the house of his widowed mother and her brother. I see also that there is a Henry James Wyley, born in Georgia, who died in Savannah, Ga. on 28 February 1921. I'm pretty sure this is a different person.

Best Wishes, Chris

* *

Oct 1, 2018, at 10:27 AM, From: Winick, Stephen

Thanks very much, Chris.

Yes, the Savannah man must be different, since if he died in 1921, he could not have recorded for Gordon five years later!

All the best, Steve

* *

From: Chris Smith

Oct 1, 2018, at 10:36 AM, Chris Smith wrote:

That will be a lesson to me not to research late at night!

Chris

* *

Kumbaya: Picking up the trail

Oct 1, 2018, at 12:04 PM, Griffin Lotson <griffinlotson@gmail.com> wrote:

Excellent Chris! This is Griffin Lotson; I'm continuing to do more research. Your research, Chris and Stephen, with the United States Library of Congress has been excellent. Some of it is of great value to history and to me. We all are going down the same path. You guys are experts at this kind of research. I'm just an amateur, historical researcher concerning this one subject and that is "Kumbaya".

It is refreshing knowing that my research that started back in 2011 matches what you discovered in 2016. At least we found the same thing, and that is, his name is Henry Wylie, aka H. Wylie, in my oral history combining it with National Archives and the census, the spelling of Henry Wylie last name changed over time.

It's not actually how his family spells the name. I have interviewed some of the family members. They are in their 90s now. They spell it not Wylie but Wylly. The younger or next generation has converted it now to Wiley. As we all know, that is nothing uncommon in certain cultures especially the Gullah Geechee culture back in the last two centuries, for several reasons. Now all of us know Henry was in Darien. As a matter of fact, Robert Winslow Gordon's wife was living in Darien before they got married. I've been in the church where they got married (St. Andrews Episcopal). That has not been publicized at all to my knowledge in any of our research. I have a copy of the marriage certificate, as well as new information that many did not know that both husband and wife are buried in the same cemetery in Darien, Georgia.

Robert died first 1961, and his lovely wife decided to send his body back to Darien after he died in Virginia, (I have a copy of the death certificate). I'm not sure when his wife came back to Darien, but one year later she died and is buried at the same location just north of Darien (in St. Andrews Cemetery).

Usually when a person chooses his/her burial site, it is usually where their heart, soul and love remain, and I think in this case it is true.

Grave marker of Robert Winslow Gordon and wife Darien, Georgia.

Many historians and researchers did not know where Robert Winslow Gordon was buried, nor did they know that Mr. Gordon and his wife live there for at least two years and, furthermore, his mother and father-in-law are buried at the same cemetery. Which gives evidence, just the opposite or contrary to some who had believed he was just passing through Darien. In fact, not only did he live there, it is where he was married also. I just wanted to give a little bit more additional information to what we have, and I'm sharing with you, others, and for the Library of Congress archives about the historical facts of this particular song "Kumbaya".

It looks like the more we research, the more we will find out through the years. Perhaps the next generation will fill in the missing pieces. I am a descendant of the Gullah Geechee culture in America. I was born in the Darien, McIntosh County area back in 1954. My grandfather Robert Lotson was born in 1882, and was recorded also in 1926 by Robert Winslow Gordon, in the Darien McIntosh County area. That's how I stumbled upon the now famous "Kumbaya" song recording. And as they say, "the rest is history" concerning my research on such a wonderful song, that's known by over a billion individuals all over the world. Thanks, Griffin 912-571-9014

On Oct 1, 2018, at 3:01 PM, Winick, Stephen wrote:

 Thanks for the photos and marriage documents, Griffin!

At the Library of Congress, we knew that Mrs. Gordon was born and raised in Darien, and that is the main reason they ended up there in the 1920s. We knew they had married there as well, and knew the date, though I had not seen the certificate before. We knew he was buried there, though, again, I haven't seen the gravestone.

Gordon wrote in a letter once that he sailed south in the S.S. City of Savannah to marry Roberta, and it's a ship we happen to have pictures of—see one at the link! I guess in 1912 he would have sailed into Savannah and gone overland from there to Darien.

https://www.loc.gov/item/2016805038/

There is a book about Robert Winslow Gordon, entitled "Good Friends and Bad Enemies," which was written by my good friend and former neighbor Debora Kodish. It's from the book that I found all these details. I assume Debora must have researched the documents and probably visited Darien when she was writing it in the 1980s. But the book came out in 1986, and I didn't know her until 1990, so we never talked about the research much. I don't see her often, since I left Philadelphia to work at the Library in 2005.

"Kumbaya" or "Come by Here" was not mentioned in Debora's book. I don't think she knew it was in there! Nor was the song found or selected as one of the items to release on an LP in the 1980s, nor was it put online with the material from the LP in the 1990s. It didn't become a famous song until the 1950s, and by then most people had forgotten it was in the collection, which is why all our research was necessary. It finally went online following my 2009 research.

We also have some extensive websites about Gordon at the Library of Congress, since he founded the archive here in 1928. They all predate my 2009 article, so no one remembered about "Kumbaya" at the time they were written. Thanks again! Stephen

From: Griffin Lotson <griffinlotson@gmail.com>

Date: Tuesday, 2 October 2018 00:11

To: "Winick, Stephen"

Cc: Chris Smith, "Cutting, Jennifer"

Subject: Re: More on Henry Wylly

Thanks Chris and Stephen, I won't trouble you guys anymore, for now anyway, but I certainly hope you don't mind if I quote some of the information you've given me?

My ultimate goal is to do a small book for advertisement and to promote our little town, Darien, Georgia. At first the little Book "Kumbaya" will be self-published and probably no more than 50 to 75 pages.

it's my understanding, and I've gotten permission from Todd Harvey that the information at the Library of Congress is public domain, and I can perhaps use some of the material each of you have done for the Library Of Congress but definitely give credit to each of you. So I am humbly asking in a very positive way, is it possible to give credit to each of you by name, for your contribution to this work "Kumbaya"?

If that's not possible, I'll just use the public domain work each of you has done through the Library of Congress's written material that you have out there now.

 Once again thanks to each of you for the wonderful work on this historical song.

****

On Oct 2, 2018, at 2:53 AM, Chris Smith wrote:

I'd be honored. "Chris Smith, independent researcher from Scotland" will describe me well enough, I think. Every success with the book! Chris

****

Oct 2, 2018, at 1:25 PM, From: Griffin Lotson <griffinlotson@gmail.com> wrote:

Thanks Stephen, this is great, I'm only using material about the family telling more of the facts. Your material and Chris's material are definitely awesome. B. B. King... yes Chris, I do have B. B. King...Come By Here Baby, "Come By Here Baby"

He recorded it as a single in 1959 and followed up on an album in 1960 (B.

B. King Wails.) Of course we all know the song was popular around that time frame (50s and 60s). As we see, B.B. King added his own twist to the song. Very popular all over the world, and in my age group, I don't think I can find one person that's a baby boomer, who has not heard of the song or phrase "Kumbaya"

Thanks, Griffin.   44

✳ ✳

Darien News and McIntosh Life Magazine

For historical significance, we thought it would be proper to give homage and the highest recognition to the first newspaper to print the new knowledge about "Kumbaya" and the first magazine to be published in the year 2017, concerning the new knowledge of the old song "Kumbaya".

We have full permission from the editor of both the newspaper and magazine to be included in this book. The editor is Kathleen Russell of the Darien News and of the McIntosh Life Magazine, summer addition 2017.

We will list in this order of the publication, in this book:

(1). Number one-Darien News, Darien, Georgia, March 16, 2017, Front Page Title: Georgia Senate declares "Come By Ya", a.k.a. Kumbaya, as Georgia Historical Song.

(2). Number two- McIntosh Life Magazine, summer issue 2017, title page 15 "Come By Ya", with a surprising nine pages of historical significance on the new and old history of the song Kumbaya.

(3). Number three-Darien News, Darien, Georgia, December 17, 2017, Front Page Title: Kumbaya makes full circle in our U.S. Capital on December 7.

(4). Number four-Darien News, Darien, Georgia, December 21, 2017, Page 4; B, Page 5-B.

From left, Darien News Chief Editor, Kathleen Russell, Mayor Hugh Hodge, City Manager, Tim Sweezey, Author of Kumbaya Book, Griffin Lotson, U.S. Senator Johnny Isakson, City Attorney, Richard Braun, City Councilman, Augustus Skeen, City Councilman, Barbara Shaw, Chamber of Commerce; Executive Director, Mandy Harrison. Dec. 7, 2017 in Washington, D.C. in Senator Isakson's Office.

From The Darien News, March 16, 2017

Georgia Senate declares "Come by Ya", aka Kumbaya, as Georgia's Historical Song

The Georgia Senate signed a resolution Monday, March 13, declaring Kumbaya, first recorded in Darien in 1926 by a Geechee descendant of slaves as Georgia's Historical Song. McIntosh County's Senator William Ligon introduced the resolution, and in attendance for the signing were City Councilman Griffin Lotson, researcher for song, Mayor Hugh Hodge, Councilman Augustus Skeen, and Darien/McIntosh Chamber of Commerce President Mandy Harrison, Lotson began his research, of the song that is internationally known as "Kumbaya", in 2012 at the direction of Sudy Leavy during the Harmonies exhibit that came to Darien. Leavy showed Lotson a listing of Library of Congress recordings done by Robert Winslow Gordon in Darien and the surrounding areas.

Tenaciously, Lotson has delved into the information provided by the Library of Congress. He received the entire cylinder of the recordings of folk songs made by Gordon, as well as the listing of each person who was recorded in the order it was recorded. Over and over Lotson listened to Wiley's recording and researched the song and found proof that the song was first recorded in Darien on April 17, 1926, by a distant relative, Henry Wiley.

At the end of each recording, Gordon had the person state his/her name, place and date. He listened to the recording just before and just after Wiley's, which was Jeff Union, who gave the same place as Darien and on the same date. Lotson has transcribed Wiley's words from his Gullah Geechee. The Gullah Geechee language is based on English, with strong influences from West African languages of the slaves who were brought to America.

"This was a slave song," Lotson explained. "We adopted the Christian religion while enslaved. We didn't know about Jesus Christ. Our plantation owners knew about Jesus Christ. We started loving Jesus. Just like any group, they start singing their own songs, putting their own words together. They created a lot of songs in those old praise houses back in the woods, because we didn't have churches.

"We worshiped freely the way we wanted to. You are singing the master's words, but you are still holding onto some of your own language and something evolved in the middle. We are the only culture in America that was birthed out of slavery. We retained most of our African culture because of the isolation on the sea islands."

The Gullah Geechee pronunciation for the English word "here" is "ya". Lotson notes that during Wiley's singing the song, he sometimes interchanges the words. Sometimes he sings "ya" and other times sing "here".

According to The Library of Congress, there was a recording of "Come by Here" by Ethel Best with a group in Raiford, Fla., in 1936. The "Kum Ba Yah" title came about after a missionary family, the Cunninghams, went to Angola in 1946 and when they returned to tour America they sang the song with the text "Kum Ba Yah".

The folk music artists began recording the song. Pete Seeger did so in 1958, as did Joan Baez's 1962 recording that took flight during the Civil Rights Movement. Lotson also notes that the Weavers from Australia recorded the song, as well as BB King, who sang his own rendition.

"Come By Ya"

Song internationally known as "Kumbaya" is Georgia's Historical Song, after being first recorded in Darien. While in the fields of plantations, in the worship houses and in the row boats on the rivers of McIntosh, African slaves and their descendants sang the song, invoking God's help...

Somebody need you Lord, come by ya.

Somebody need you Lord, come by ya.

O, Lord, come by ya.

I need you Lord, come by ya.

Sinner need you Lord, come by ya.

Sinner need you Lord, come by ya. Oh, Lord, come by ya.

The Gullah Geechee people of this coastal community, as well as other coastal communities of Georgia and South Carolina continued to sing this song, known today as "Kumbaya", or "Come By Here", or as recorded for the very first time in Darien in 1926 by Robert Gordon with Henry Wiley singing "Come by ya". In March, the Georgia General Assembly named the song as Georgia's Historical Song.

There is a winding story about just exactly how that came about. In 1912, a Harvard professor, Robert Winslow Gordon, who had the passion to document the depth and variety of the American folk song, just happened to meet and marry Roberta Porter Paul of Darien. In 1917, the Gordon's and their daughter, Roberta, moved to California for Robert to teach English at the University of California at Berkeley. His interests grew in folk song, folk belief, and technology, as reported by the American Folklife Center at the Library of Congress in Washington, D.C.

He returned to Harvard and in 1925-1926 planned a trip around the United States to make a recorded collection of American folk songs. He had accumulated funding for the project from Harvard and donations of equipment from Eastman, Ford and Edison. It is reported that by Christmas of 1925, the separation from his family was taking a toll financially and emotionally. So, the family decided to move to Darien, where Gordon set up his field station.

Debora G. Kodish writes about the Gordon's life in Darien. "Gordon felt that he occupied a special position in the Darien black community. He had earned the trust and friendship of several local blacks, among them W.M. Givens, whose niece was sometimes employed by the Gordon's.

"One day she came running terrified, into their home. Her uncle had been bitten by a poisonous snake. Gordon rushed back with her, put a tourniquet on the man's leg, cut the bite and sucked out the venom. Billy Givens was soon walking again, and Gordon had earned a friend for life—a friend who also happened to be a fine singer.

"All of Gordon's Georgia informants lived within a day's drive of Darien, for Gordon did not have enough cash to buy gasoline most of the time and was obliged to return to the station where he had credit. Nor did he always take the car on field trips; he knew the countryside for 15 miles around Darien from his long walks."

Kodish reported that Gordon desired a steadier source of income, and since he had conducted extensive research at the Library of Congress, he presented his dream of a chance to collect, examine, and theorize American folk song to Earl Engel, who was the chief of the Music Division at the Library of Congress in the fall of 1926. Engel had a dream of creating a graduate institute for the study of musicology, with a national center for the collection and study of folk music. So, the project was on. By 1928, Gordon became the director of the Archive of American Folk Song.

For the first year, Gordon stayed in Darien, where Kodish reports that he collected shouts, rowing songs, reels, and rags and turning songs that held the most significant importance in the study of American folk song and the special importance of the starting and spreading for folk songs. In 1929, the Gordon family moved to Washington, and Gordon installed his archive in the southwest corner of the Library's attic.

Now, The Robert Winslow Gordon Collection, 1922-1932, of Folk-Songs of America contains thousands of recorded songs, letters and texts from across America. And in the collection are 555 songs he acquired while living in Darien between 1926 and 1928, including the first recording of "Come By Ya" of Henry Wiley on April 17, 1926. That very fact was not arrived upon without a lot of digging and tenacity by Darien Gullah Geechee descendant Griffin Lotson to determine who sang the song, when it was sung, and where it was sung. And with his persistence, the naming of the song as Georgia's Historical Song was accomplished.

Lotson began his research in 2012 at the direction of Sudy Leavy, while the Harmonies exhibit was in Darien. She showed Lotson a listing of Library of Congress recordings done by Gordon in Darien and the surrounding area. Lotson traveled to the Library several times to delve into the information that is available there. The Library gave him the entire cylinder of the recordings made by Gordon in the Darien area, as well as the listing of each person who was recorded in the order they were recorded.

Over, and over, and over, Lotson listened to Wiley singing "Come by Ya" to determine the exact words. He was also able to determine the proof of when and who recorded each one because Gordon had each person state his/her name, place and date at the end of each recording. He listened to the recording just before and just after Wiley's, which was the recording of Jeff Union, who gave the same place as Darien and on the same date.

Lotson explained the Gullah Geechee customs and dialect. "This was a slave song. We adopted the Christian religion while enslaved. We didn't know about Jesus Christ. Our plantation owners knew about Jesus Christ. We started loving Jesus. Just like any group, they started singing their own songs, putting their own words together. They created a lot of songs in those old praise houses back in the woods, because they didn't have churches.

They worshiped freely the way they wanted too. They were singing the master's words, but they were still holding onto some of their own language and something evolved in the middle. We are the only culture in America that was birthed out of slavery. We retained most of our African culture, because of the isolation of the sea islands. The Gullah Geechee pronunciation for the English word "here" is "ya". Lotson noted his distant relative, Henry Wiley, interchanged the words in the recording. Sometimes he sang "ya", and other times he sang "here".

According to The Library of Congress, there was a recording of "Come by Here" by Ethel Best, with a group in Raiford, Fla., in 1936. The "Kum Ba Yah" title came about after a missionary family, the Cunninghams, went to Angola in 1946 and when they returned to tour America, they sang the song with the phrase "Kum Ba Yah".

The folk music artists began recording the song. Pete Seeger did so in 1958. Joan Baez's recording took flight in 1962, during the Civil Rights Movement. Many, many other groups recorded the song. All over the world the song has been sung...in churches and around campfires.

So, on Monday, March 13, 2017, the resolution was signed on the Georgia Senate floor declaring "Come By Ya", aka "Kumbaya", as Georgia's Historical Song, thanks to the help of Senator William Ligon, who introduced the

legislation.

The Darien News Dec. 17, 2017, Kumbaya makes full circle in our U.S. Capitol on Dec. 7th

By Kathleen Russell

Kumbaya, my Lord. Kumbaya.
Come by here, my Lord. Come by here.

First District Congressman Buddy Carter stood on the floor of the U.S. House of Representatives to recognize the importance of the song, Kumbaya, to this nation and the world. Quietly sitting in the gallery of the massive and daunting hall were members of the City Council of Darien and staff for the recognition of the song that originated on Georgia's coast and was first recorded in Darien.

Congressman Carter stated: "I rise today to recognize a very important song to the history of the State of Georgia, Kumbaya. The first known recording of Kumbaya took place in 1926 near Darien, Georgia. The original name of the song was "Come by Here", but now the song is internationally known as "Kumbaya".

"While the exact origin of the song is uncertain, scholars believe it originated with the Gullah Geechee people, who are descendants of enslaved African Americans of the sea islands of the coastal regions of Georgia. It is largely believed that the song is a plea for God's intervention for this group of African Americans, asking Him to relieve them from a number of different hard times in the community...a sick family member, the oppression, and more.

Robert Winslow Gordon, staff member and original founder of the Library of Congress Archive of Folk Songs, was temporarily living in Georgia in 1926 (Darien) and tape the first recording of Kumbaya. The wax cylinder recording No. A139 is still located in the Library of Congress today. He recorded a person in the Gullah Geechee community named H. Wiley, who sang the lyrics. "Need you, Lord. Come by here. Somebody need you, Lord, come by here.'

This recording is one of the earliest items located in the Library of Congress Archives of Folk Song. Today, Robert Winslow Gordon is buried in Darien, home of that first recording of Kumbaya. Scholars think that 'Come by here' simply sounds like "Kumbaya" to some listeners--a non-existent word at the time that evolved into the song that we have here today. Other scholars think that the original song was not even 'Come by here', but instead, 'Come by ya'.

Since that time, the song has spread through our nation and the world. Recordings can even be found and sung by Americans throughout all different times in our nation's history. There are 1930s recordings from central Texas and in Florida; and while many Americans were finding solace during the Jim Crow period in the 1950s and 1960s; Kumbaya was sung by Pete Seegar, as well as Peter, Paul, and Mary, and Joan Baez. The song has even been traced to Angola, transported by missionaries.

Even today, Kumbaya means something different to different groups of people...,but we should never forget the original meaning of the song and who we believe were the original creators of the song, the Gullah Geechee people...

As a result of the Gullah Geechee people creating the song of Kumbaya, they have been a significant force not only in the First Congressional District of Georgia, but across the world and throughout American history. To recognize just how widespread this song has become, the Georgia General Assembly passed a resolution stating the impact this song has had on our state of Georgia.

I hope you all will join me in our nation's Capital by also recognizing the importance of this song. I am very proud that it originated in the First Congressional District of Georgia. It is an honor to have members of the Gullah Geechee people here in the House today..."

At the end of the speech, Darien's Mayor Hugh Hodge, Mayor Pro Tem Griffin Lotson (who is a Geechee descendant of slaves and tenaciously discovered the song was first recorded in Darien and brought forth that information to the community, state and nation), Council members Barbara Shaw and Augustus Skeen, along with City Manager Tim Sweezey, City Attorney Richard Braun, Darien-McIntosh Chamber President Mandy Harrison, Library of Congress Director of the American Folklife Center, Betsy Peterson, and Library of Congress Folklife Specialist, Todd Harvey, and Gullah Geechee Corridor Commission, Director Heather Hodges met Rep. Carter on the steps of the U.S. Capitol, where they sang "Kumbaya" in unison and posed for photos on the momentous occasion for the City of Darien.

That evening on nationally televised news, it was announced that there was a "Kumbaya" in Washington, D.C. It was not the actual reporting of the recognition of the origin of the Kumbaya by the Gullah Geechee slave descendants asking God to "come by here", as was reported on CSPAN in the House of Representatives on the morning of Dec. 7, 2017.

The newscast was concerned by the impending government shutdown. If the members of the U.S. House of Representatives and U.S. Senate did not vote that day, there would be a government shutdown. The broadcast showed President Donald Trump and Vice President Mike Pence sitting in the Oval Office with Speaker of the House Paul Ryan, House Minority Leader Nancy Pelosi, Senate Majority Leader Mitch McConnell and Senate Minority Leader Chuck Schumer discussing the need for the passage of House Joint Resolution 123 to continue appropriations for the fiscal year 2018 from Dec. 8 to Dec. 22, to prevent a government shutdown. It was a "come by here" moment in the nation. By 4:48 p.m., the House of Representatives passed the resolution 235 to 193, with Rep. Carter voting in the affirmative. Then the Senate voted to pass the resolution.

Darien News December 21, 2017, Two Darien men bring "Kumbaya" to be worlds' song asking for divine intervention

By Kathleen Russell

On Dec. 7, our congressman, Rep. Buddy Carter, recognized the importance of the song Kumbaya which pleads for God's presence, to the nation and the world, as a song that was originated by the Gullah-Geechee people and first recorded in Darien on April 17, 1926.

It has taken the work of two men to bring this about: Darien's Griffin Lotson, a Gullah-Geechee descendant, has been researching the first recording since 2012 to determine its origin, and Robert Winslow Gordon, who lived in Darien, recorded the song and became the first director of the American Folklife Archive at the Library of Congress in 1928. He and his wife, Roberta Paul Gordon, a native of McIntosh County, are buried in St. Andrew's Cemetery.

On Dec. 8, Todd Harvey, Library of Congress American Folklife Center Reference Librarian, afforded Darien-McIntosh Chamber of Commerce President Mandy Harrison and The Darien News' Kathleen Russell several hours of sharing information about Gordon, his expansive work, and the significance of his particular recording of "Kumbaya" in Darien. We met in the American Folklife Reading Room in the Library of Congress Jefferson

Building located across from the U.S. Capitol.

Harvey began talking about the first documented recording of Kumbaya, "In 1926 in Darien, Georgia. A man named Henry Wylie sang the song into the microphone of a wax cylinder recorder. Operating the machine was folklorist and ethnographer, Robert Winslow Gordon. A few years later, Gordon became the first Director of the Archives of American Folk Song, as it was called at that time, and he brought with him his collection of wax cylinders that included Henry Wylie's recording. That recording was the first recorded documentation of the song, Come By Here, which became the world-famous song, Kumbaya.

Equally important, I think, is that its placement in the location signaled that Gullah-Geechee was one of the foundational cultures of the American patchwork," Harvey noted. Gordon was a folklorist and ethnographer, who had a career in a lot of different spaces and places when they hired him with a Rockefeller grant that the Library of Congress received," Harvey said.

Gordon majored in English literature at Harvard and taught English there, when he met and married his wife in 1912. In 1914, they had a daughter, Roberta, when they were living in Cambridge. Then he became an assistant professor of English at the University of California at Berkeley in 1918. During the seven years in California, Gordon collected and recorded numerous sea songs and shanties. During that time, he began writing a column for the pulp magazine Adventure, "Old Songs That Men Have Sung". He printed songs that readers requested and invited additional texts.

At some point in the early 20th century, the Library of Congress got into its DNA that we are building a universal collection of knowledge and wisdom. It was not just a library for the Congress anymore...It was bigger than that. The copyright office was put here in the 1870s or so, and we were doing great in the knowledge department, but wisdom was lacking. So they founded the Archive of Folksong, because they knew the voices of ordinary people were we get wisdom. So there were other thoughts, traditional culture, and traditional music was kind of being erased by mass media that was starting to grow. You think about the 1920s radio...between 1925 and 1935; everybody had a radio. Things really happened fast, just like we are seeing now on the web.

Harvey continued, "Gordon was brought in as the head of the archive that was founded and put into the music division. He was a good field worker and worked in Darien for a long time. He also recorded music of the upland South, North Carolina, banjo music, and Scotch-Irish music.

Gordon wanted to be in the field. That was his passion. These wax cylinders were what he had to work with at the time." Harvey demonstrated with a model wax cylinder, by placing a blank cylinder onto the spindle of the machine. There is a microphone on the machine to record the sounds, and as the cylinder spins it cuts, just like a disc would do.

Gordon brought with him to the Library of Congress to begin the foundation of the American Folklife Achieve a collection of almost 1,000 cylinders, 10,000 or more of song texts given by readers of articles he wrote in Adventure magazine. And, he had collected thousands of song versions from old camp-meetings and revival songbooks. Gordon was said to be a pioneer among the folklorists during the 1920s and 1930s.

Harvey continued, "His wife typed the songs (that were written in his column, 'Songs Old Men Have Sung'), and they are bound. We have the original song texts people would send in. It is an amazing resource of folksongs...everything you can imagine. Things like this are pretty unique." There were songs about the Titanic, as well as songs from the 1860s and 1870s. It is just a snapshot of song. The original handwritten letters are archived down in the stacks (basement where Harvey toured us). This is just one thing he left to us." Harvey brought out one of Gordon's books that included songs from 1921 to 1930s, typewritten by his wife.

Another thing that Gordon left us was the collection of songsters--a little collection of songbooks that the people in the 19th century would have had, which would be inappropriate today. The books included composed songs, as well as recitations of Shakespeare or Wordsworth. It was an important documentation of community life in small communities and how they passed things down," Harvey said.

He brought out the list of inventory of the Gordon cylinders, including the page noting Henry Wylie recording "Somebody need you Lord, come by here". "Before Griffin showed up at the Library of Congress, this is what we knew. I think we might have done some research, 'Oh my gosh, that's Kumbaya', but the details we did not know. With bits of information, you can see how hard it is to figure out what the songs are," Harvey said, noting that it is so important that the Library of Congress staff communicate with communities.

Through Griffin Lotson's five-year search for the details, more knowledge was brought forth to the point that the song was identified as Georgia's Historical Song last March and is recognized now in the U.S. House of Representatives.

"Come by 'ya, my Lord. Come by 'ya..."

For the first time never seen before publicly a photo of the original singer of Kumbaya Henry Wiley This historical photo has never been revealed to the public.

Henry Wiley

Henry was considered to be a mulatto, this is a persons by definition that looks almost like an America white person. Mulatto: In America, the offspring of one white parent and one black parent. Back in time, antebellum Days in slavery, 19th century and Early part of the 20th century in America the term mulatto was more of a slang word for African-American Black* Persons that looks almost white. The English term and spelling mulatto is derived from the Spanish and Portuguese mulato. The origin of mulato is uncertain, though it may derive from Portuguese mula (from the Latin mūlus), meaning mule, the hybrid offspring of a horse and a donkey.

In America in the 21st-century the word mulatto is almost unmentionable, and not use at all under normal circumstances, times have changed, thank God.

Great Escape

Henry Wiley daring escape July 26, 1926 from Georgia to South Carolina, with the help of a family member he left secretly from the prison camp location in Darien, Georgia, and escape in an automobile through the back roads all the way to South Carolina, Change his name from Henry Wiley to Ernest Henry Anderson where he live a successful life from the end of 1926 up until his death in 1964, he died at the age of 65. It took the Author of this book nearly 10 years to uncover this hidden deep family secret and now this much we can present to the world, there is more that can be told........

Henry Wiley true story of the Kumbaya original singer from the first recording 1926.

Un-mark grave of Henry Wiley buried in South Carolina, located to the left of the family graves seen in photo.

John Wiley Anderson, Henry Wiley only surviving son, photo July 22, 2020

Family members that was interviewed July 22, 2020

John Anderson, Henry Anderson Johnson and great great granddaughter Toney L. king

Interviewed his other in-laws, Miss Martha Roberson, Henry remarried Martha's aunt Eva Palmer in SC, they all lived in the same house, in the other photo is Marie Wiley Riley.

THE UNSUNG HEROES

Unsung heroes from Georgia, that we conducted oral interviews with that provided information that had never been known in nearly 100 years concerning the history of Kumbaya: Matilda Wiley Jonathan Wiley, Anita (Jackson, Wiley) White, without the names above, the hidden mysteries and history of Kumbaya would be forever last in time. A special thank you to each of them for their contribution.

Kumbaya: Summing Up and Thanks

In this book we have gathered information more than any other time in history to dispel some of the mysteries of this fascinating song called "Kumbaya", but it is clear to me there's much more information that we still can obtain by searching the archives that are already placed at our disposal. Author Deborah Kodish has done some very significant work and printed some of that information in a book "Good friends and Bad Enemies", (Robert Winslow Gordon and the study of American folksong) by Deborah Kodish.

She has done what I have accomplished in this book "Kumbaya" and that is, get real information directly from the source. In her book she dedicated Chapter 6, a total of 32 pages of information specifically from and within the City of Darien, and surrounding areas, which help solidify my research, and it is a known fact that the song was recorded in Darien, and I'm giving special credit to Miss Kodish for some of her research.

Now we know, contrary to what some other historians had doubted in the past, but now we have specific proof that the oldest known recording in the world was completed and recorded in Darien. This information comes exclusively and specifically from two gentlemen, and we thank them: Mr. Henry Wiley a.k.a. "H. Wylie" who actually sang the song in 1926, and Mr. Robert Winslow Gordon, the gentleman who recorded the song in 1926.

A special thanks to Mr. Robert Winslow Gordon, who did the recording and documented his research, and preserved the history of his finding that is now placed in the archives of the Library of Congress in Washington, D.C. and Virginia. Both of these locations I have visited and personally had an opportunity to research some of these documents and recordings. The Library of Congress has the largest collection of folklore cultures from countries from around the world, and in particular, this specific information concerning the world's most popular song, "Kumbaya", that now has been proven, was, in fact, recorded in Darien, Georgia.

In this book we are preserving the history for future generations, about this fascinating worldwide song that's known by over one billion individuals all over the planet.

As we all continue to find out more about this fascinating song, perhaps each of us reading this book and all of the historians will take the time to read all 3,785 letters that Mr. Robert Winslow Gordon has very carefully placed in a collection at the Library Congress in Washington, D.C.

As we approach the end of the first edition of the world's first book on a simple but yet powerful song and phase called "Kumbaya", it still fascinates me after all these many years, that the word and song has been used now very powerfully since the 1950s, as we have approached 92 years of history as of this year 2019, the word "Kumbaya", or the song "Kumbaya" there has not been one movie titled, not one book written, until now, nationally or internationally, on such a profoundly powerful song or phrase "Kumbaya", that is known by over one billion individuals worldwide.

Never use the word "Kumbaya" negatively again

A legendary civil rights icon, Vinson Harding, was a speech writer and close friend of Dr. Martin Luther King Jr., said in his remembrance of the song Kumbaya how he could never laugh when others would speak in a negative way about Kumbaya. Vincent Harding tells a compelling true story that touches my heart concerning this powerful song that has changed the lives of many.

Now I follow the same thought pattern of Mr. Harding, knowing the original true meaning of the song as it was back in 1926. Now for some in the 21st-century, mainly in America, I'm sure it is beginning to spread worldwide at a very slow pace. I hope, the new negative way of using such a beautiful, lovely peaceful song, now to make fun of this one word or song "Kumbaya" will come to an end.

I, for one, will hope to never use the word "Kumbaya" negatively again, or to make fun of "Come By Ya", "Come By Here" aka "Kumbaya", mainly because I know the true history of the song, I'm also somewhat sympathetic to those that ignorantly or unknowingly use this song or word for negative purposes. I truly believe most do this because they don't know the real history of the song. One song or word "Kumbaya" can change the way a person thinks of life.

We now know that in a positive way the song was used during the civil rights movement in America in times past in the 1950s and 60s, when individuals lost their lives, just to help individuals register to vote, primarily good citizens that happened to be African-American and White. When these volunteers lost their lives, the remaining volunteer workers who had traveled to the deep South, just to help out heard the bad news of the death of their fellow volunteer workers, Just by assisting individuals to register to vote, their hearts were broken, and some were even fearful that their own lives might be taken.

Yes, when it seemed like all would be lost and the whole room was silent because of the horror of some that had been killed...Someone broke out and started singing the song Come By Here, Lord, Come By Here; after that song, they all decided not to leave but to continue to fight the good fight of faith, by continuing to assist individuals to register for voting, (The Power of one song). This book and the author Griffin Lotson, could never use the word "Kumbaya" negatively again.

Volunteer Service for History

The author, voluntarily served as the lead consultant and choreographer working with The Atlanta Symphony Orchestra ensemble to compose music specifically and directly from the original recording of "Kumbaya" 1926, singing with a community choir with members throughout the city of Darien and McIntosh County, at an overflow crowd of participants, at the Archie Myers auditorium.

The author also have the pleasure of voluntarily serving as the lead consultant and choreographer working with the Geechee Gullah Ring Shouters, which was the first group in the world to record as a group the original words of Henry Wiley in the original dialect of the Gullah Geechee's, from the words on the original recording of "Kumbaya "from 1926. The United States of America's Library of Congress has authenticated the Geechee Gullah Ring Shouters recording of the song "Kumbaya", by placing the recording near the end of a podcast, where the group is singing in the dialect as it was originally sung by Henry Wylie in 1926, the world's oldest known recording.

The Geechee Gullah Ring Shouters Perform

The author voluntarily served as the lead consultant working with the National Recording Registry, placing the entry of the sound "Kumbaya" from the year 1926.

Each year, the National Recording Registry at the Library of Congress chooses 25 recordings showcasing the range and diversity of American recorded sound - heritage in order to increase preservation awareness.

The author voluntarily served as the International lead consultant working with Gullah Geechee's and others to have the song Kumbaya accepted as the International Anthem for the Gullah Geechee culture and or worldwide African Diaspora and its descendants.

It is the hope that by writing this book, we all would look at this song, this movement in a different light. Perhaps now we can start going back to its original meaning of the song of "Needing Divine Help', needing togetherness, needing love, and unity, our greatest hope at the conclusion of this book, along with the fact of being the first book to give the real history of an old song that has positive meaning to so many of us all over the world, we hope this book will give a sense of appreciation for this great

song we all call "Kumbaya".

To hear and see more about "Kumbaya"

(To hear the Robert Winslow Gordon recording of Henry Wylly singing "Kumbaya", type in AUDIO RECORDING Come by Here Kumbaya) :

Or on the internet just type in:

(On the Folklife Today Podcast: "Kumbaya")

Special recognition to all the organizations that made this Book possible and went the extra mile to support Griffin Lotson and this book "Kumbaya":

Georgia Department of Economic Development, Tourism Division
Darien McIntosh County Chamber of Commerce
City of Darien, Georgia
Sams Memorial Community Economic Development, Nonprofit
Georgia State Senate,
National NAACP Kumbaya Resolution
New York Times
The Darien News, Darien, Georgia
BBC News Worldwide
Georgia Public Broadcasting
United States of America, Library of Congress
Gullah Geechee Cultural Heritage
United States of America Congress
West Africa Serra Leone

Timeline cycle of Kumbaya

1800s Timeline cycle of Kumbaya and its meaning: Beginning time of the song unknown, first original writer unknown, probably in the 1800s.

1926. First known recording in the world, the original meaning of the song Kumbaya, was a call to God for help, divine intervention.

1950s-1980's. Meaning change for many, to a call for unity working and coming together for peaceful loving circumstances.

1980s-to present day 21st century, The song Kumbaya meaning experience another change, where some individuals use it in a negative way condescending way by many but not all.

2019. A positive reversal of the original meeting of the song "Kumbaya", of which was positive for over 50 years, then started turning to be negative or condescending, but now present day, it is turning back to a very positive word and song from its original days. With this new book "Kumbaya", and with the help of you the readers, we now begin an international movement toward bringing this song "Kumbaya" and word back to its original meaning of "A call for help from God and or a call for unity working together for peaceful and lovable communication".

2020. First time never seen before publicly, a photo of the original singer of Kumbaya "Henry Wiley". This historical photo has never been revealed to the public until now.

THE LIBRARY OF CONGRESS
101 INDEPENDENCE AVENUE, S.E.
WASHINGTON, D.C. 20540-4610

AMERICAN FOLKLIFE CENTER
202-707-5510 (Voice)
202-707-2076 (FAX)
folklife@loc.gov (Email)

September 30, 2016

Dear Mr. Lotson,

Thank you for your visit last month and for the productive subsequent conversations. I wish to express interest and support for your project to document Gullah Geechee culture in and around Darien, Georgia.

As you know, some of the first recordings made by what is now the American Folklife Center were made in Darien. Robert Winslow Gordon recorded the singing repertoire of African-Americans, including what may be the first recordings of "Come By Here."

Understanding Gullah Geechee culture today is of national importance. Finding and recording the memories of individuals who were recorded by Gordon would be especially useful for Library of Congress researchers.

I look forward to further discussions as your work progresses. The Center can be helpful in the planning, execution, and archiving phases of your project.

Best Regards,

Todd Harvey
Acquisitions Coordinator
American Folklife Center
Library of Congress

Mr. Griffin Lotson,
Gullah Geechee Historian
1033 Poppell Dr.
P.O. Box 1549
Darien, Georgia

Kumbaya makes 300 year connection with the Ring Shout in West Africa Serra Leone

https://www.bbc.co.uk/sounds/play/p06y0l33

The State of Georgia's First State Historical Song in nearly 300 years of Georgia history "Kumbaya"

(Left to right) 1. Lester G. Jackson State Senator, 2. William Ligon, Jr. State Senator, 3. Hugh "Bubba" Hodge, city of Darien, Mayor, 4. Augustus "Bubba" Skeen, city of Darien Councilman, 5. Casey Cagle, Lieutenant Governor of Georgia, 6. Mandy Harrison, Executive Director Darien-McIntosh County Chamber of Commerce, 7. (Center) Griffin Lotson, Mayor Pro Tem, City of Darien. Photo 2017 at State Capital.

Cover Photo: Butler Island Plantation

Butler Island Plantation is a former rice plantation located on Butler Island on the Altamaha River delta just South of down town Darien, Georgia. The Butler Island Plantation was originally owned by Major Pierce Butler (1744–1822) one of the signers of the original United States Constitution. The plantation now is managed by the Georgia Department of Natural Resources, along with a lease agreement with the city of Darien Georgia.

The Huston House located on Butler Island, Darien, Georgia, and was constructed in 1927 by Colonel T.L. Huston, a former co-owner of the New York Yankees. Butler Island, was originally a rice plantation dating to the late 1700s, was converted to a dairy and lettuce farm by Col. Huston in the 20th century. After Huston death in 1938, the property was purchased by tobacco heir R. J. Reynolds, Jr. The parcel is currently owned by the Department of Natural Resources Wildlife Division.

The Rice mill chimney is all that remains of the enslaved labor on the Butler Island Plantation. The chimney was built in 1832–1833; this lasting landmark is 75 ft., tall brick chimney, now we call this sit:

"A Living Monument and Testament, of the Largest Slaves Sale in America's History"

We now have come to call this site the "Weeping Days"-"Weeping Times".

The real history of "Kumbaya" is located in this same area, in the City of Darien, county of McIntosh Georgia. The first known recording in the world of Kumbaya, was recorded less than 1 mile from Butler Island

For re-order or more information
Email: Kumbayabook@gmail.com
(912) 571-9014

Mailing address:
Kumbaya Book
P. O. Box 1549
Darien, GA 31305

NOTE PAGE

www.ingramcontent.com/pod-product-compliance
Lightning Source LLC
Chambersburg PA
CBHW031152250726
48655CB00002B/946